The Freudian Wish

Also from Westphalia Press
westphaliapress.org

The Idea of the Digital University

Dialogue in the Roman-Greco World

The History of Photography

International or Local Ownership?: Security Sector Development in Post-Independent Kosovo

Lankes, His Woodcut Bookplates

Opportunity and Horatio Alger

The Role of Theory in Policy Analysis

The Little Confectioner

Non Profit Organizations and Disaster

The Idea of Neoliberalism: The Emperor Has Threadbare Contemporary Clothes

Social Satire and the Modern Novel

Ukraine vs. Russia: Revolution, Democracy and War: Selected Articles and Blogs, 2010-2016

James Martineau and Rebuilding Theology

A Strategy for Implementing the Reconciliation Process

Issues in Maritime Cyber Security

Understanding Art

Homeopathy

Fishing the Florida Keys

Iran: Who Is Really In Charge?

Contracting, Logistics, Reverse Logistics: The Project, Program and Portfolio Approach

The Thomas Starr King Dispute

Springfield: The Novel

Lariats and Lassos

Mr. Garfield of Ohio

The French Foreign Legion

War in Syria

Ongoing Issues in Georgian Policy and Public Administration

Growing Inequality: Bridging Complex Systems, Population Health and Health Disparities

Designing, Adapting, Strategizing in Online Education

Gunboat and Gun-runner

Pacific Hurtgen: The American Army in Northern Luzon, 1945

Natural Gas as an Instrument of Russian State Power

New Frontiers in Criminology

Feeding the Global South

The Freudian Wish and its Place in Ethics

by Edwin B. Holt

WESTPHALIA PRESS
An Imprint of Policy Studies Organization

The Freudian Wish and its Place in Ethics
All Rights Reserved © 2018 by Policy Studies Organization

Westphalia Press
An imprint of Policy Studies Organization
1527 New Hampshire Ave., NW
Washington, D.C. 20036
info@ipsonet.org

ISBN-13: 978-1-63391-636-4
ISBN-10: 1-63391-636-7

Cover design by Jeffrey Barnes:
jbarnesbook.design

Daniel Gutierrez-Sandoval, Executive Director
PSO and Westphalia Press

Updated material and comments on this edition
can be found at the Westphalia Press website:
www.westphaliapress.org

THE FREUDIAN WISH

AND

ITS PLACE IN ETHICS

By

EDWIN B. HOLT

NEW YORK
HENRY HOLT AND COMPANY
1916

COPYRIGHT, 1915,
BY
HENRY HOLT AND COMPANY

Published November, 1915

PRINTED IN THE UNITED STATES

To
L. H. E.

PREFACE

THE problem of good conduct, both in practice and in ethical theory, ought to receive some clarification, one would suppose, from a science that studies the mind and the will in their actual operation. If in the past psychology has not materially contributed to this problem, it is possibly owing to the incompetence of psychology to tell us much that is either true or useful about the essential nature of mind or will, or of the soul. I believe that such has been the case, and that now for the first time, and largely owing to the insight of Dr. Sigmund Freud, a view of the will has been gained which can be of real service to ethics. In presenting this I shall disregard the current comments on Freud, which have become so familiar, for he deserves neither the furious dispraise nor the frantic worship which have been accorded him. He is a man of genius, simply, more sagacious and more perspicacious than his detractors and far more sane than many of his followers. In my opinion both of these have failed to emphasize that for which Freud is most significant.

The idea has gone abroad that the term 'Freudian' is somehow synonymous with 'sexual,' and that to read Freud's own works would be fairly to immerse oneself in the licentious and the illicit. This belief, which makes the mention of Freud so alluring to some and so disconcerting to others, is as ill-founded as it is widespread. It is true that the unco prudish would experience a *mauvais quart-d'heure* if they ever permitted themselves to read Freud on the source and significance of prudishness, but it is also true that the pruriently curious would be baffled to the point of tears if they were to search in Freud for a stimulus to their own peculiar type of imagination. In short, this talk of the 'sexual' in connection with Freud is merely another instance of that infallible instinct of the cheap press and the vulgar mind to seize on unessentials, whether for praise or for blame, and to leave the main fabric unscanned.

Now Freud's contribution to science is notable, and in my opinion epoch-making, for a reason which has hardly ever been mentioned. And this reason is that he has given to the science of mind a 'causal category': or, to put it less academically, he has given us a key to the explanation of mind.

It is the first key which psychology has ever had which fitted, and moreover I believe it is the only one that psychology will ever need. Although of course these two statements would be savagely disputed by the comfortably established professors of an earlier school, who are a bit mystified by Freud and suffer from the uncomfortable apprehension that he is doing something to them; they know not quite what. And in fact he is, for he is making them look hopelessly incompetent. This key to the mind, which Freud calls the 'wish,' is the subject of the present volume. And we shall consider more particularly the bearing which this wish-psychology may have on ethics. For this is a matter which Freud himself has said little about, and one which affords, I think, very interesting and practically useful conclusions.

In the Supplement is reprinted a short paper, which first appeared in the *Journal of Philosophy, Psychology, and Scientific Methods*, and which undertakes to show the cardinal importance of this same 'wish,' there, however, called the 'specific response relation,' in the general field of psychology.

E. B. H.

CONTENTS

CHAPTER		PAGE
I	THE DOCTRINE OF THE 'WISH'	3
II	THE PHYSIOLOGY OF WISHES; AND THEIR INTEGRATION	47
III	THE WISH IN ETHICS	100
IV	SOME BROADER ASPECTS OF THE FREUDIAN ETHICS	134
	SUPPLEMENT—RESPONSE AND COGNITION	153

THE FREUDIAN WISH

CHAPTER I

THE DOCTRINE OF THE 'WISH'

The Freudian psychology is based on the doctrine of the 'wish,' just as physical science is based, to-day, on the concept of function. Both of these are what may be called dynamic concepts, rather than static; they envisage natural phenomena not as things but as processes, and largely to this fact is due their preëminent explanatory value. Through the 'wish' the 'thing' aspect of mental phenomena, the more substantive 'content of consciousness,' becomes somewhat modified and reinterpreted. This 'wish,' which as a concept Freud does not analyze, includes all that would commonly be so classed, and also whatever would be called impulse, tendency, desire, purpose, attitude, and the like; not including, however, any emotional components thereof. Freud also acknowledges the existence of what he calls 'negative wishes'; and these are not fears but negative purposes. An exact definition of the 'wish' is that it is *a course of action* which some mechanism of the body is *set* to carry out, whether it actually does so or does not. All emotions, as well as the feelings of pleasure and displeasure, are separable from the 'wishes'; and this precludes any thought of a merely hedonistic psychology. The wish is any purpose or project for *a course of action*, whether it is being merely entertained by the mind or is being actually executed; a distinction which is really of little importance. We shall do well if we consider this wish to be, as in fact it is, dependent on a *motor attitude* of the physical body, which goes over into overt action and *conduct* when the wish is carried into execution.

Now some wishes are compatible while others are antagonistic, and it is in the interplay of wishes that one finds the text of the entire Freudian psychology. It is a dynamic psychology, utterly, although Freud says little as to the energy which drives the machinery. One will best, I think, not hypothecate to this end any such thing as 'psychic energy,' but look rather, for the energy so expended, in the nervous system, which does, in fact, establish the motor attitudes and their conflicts, and does actuate the muscles to the performance

THE DOCTRINE OF THE 'WISH' 5

of conduct. Wishes conflict when they would lead the body into opposed lines of conduct, for it is clear that the body cannot at the same time, say, lie abed and yet be hurrying to catch a train; and this is the source of conflict in all cases, even those where the actual physical interference is too subtle to be readily detected. It is clear, then, that of two opposed attitudes only one can be carried into effect; the other is 'suppressed.' We shall later see how the suppressed wish can be still entertained, and whether it can exert influence. Freud finds that many familiar phenomena, such as wit, dreams, lapses of memory, and so forth, are the work of wish-conflicts. And with these we come to a more concrete matter.

Many dreams are quite obviously the pure realization of wishes; the person does, in his dream, what he deep-down wishes to do, but has been prevented from doing when awake by the cares and importunities of the daily routine, or by some other obstacle. The dreams of children are usually of activities which the mother or nurse had forbidden during the day; so, too, it is said, the dreams of saints are of rites and practices which the saint yearns for, but for which a prosaic world provides too little scope. It is clear enough that all such dreams are dictated by wishes. It would be a most pertinent question, however, to ask how the necessary scenery is provided, the mountain of sweets for the child, and for the saint the rapturous vision of the Kingdom of the Blest. Freud, I think, has not enlightened us here; but we have from other sources sufficient indications that the mechanisms of perception and of will are alike in structure, so far indeed as they are not identically the same mechanism, to make probable the supposition that 'wishes' can count on the cooperation of the, here deceptive, 'senses.'

Such dreams are in any case, so far as their motive and cause goes, clear products of the wish. But many other dreams, the nonsensical and the horrible, are not so readily explained. Herr Pepi, a medical student, was called in the morning when it was time to get up and go to the hospital for his daily rounds. He roused up, but fell asleep again, and dreamed of himself as lying in one of the beds at the hospital; at the head of the bed was one of the official cards reading—"Pepi H. Student of medicine. Age 22 years." Then in his dream he said to himself: "Well, since I'm al-

THE DOCTRINE OF THE 'WISH' 7

ready at the hospital I don't have to get up to go there." Then he turned over and slept on. This dream, while nonsensical, still clearly expresses the wish of one who wants to lie abed in the morning. But it provided an excuse for lying abed, and this shows that more than this single wish was at work to produce the dream. This other factor was clearly another wish—to be at the hospital as duty required; and this wish, weaker than the first, was strong enough to transfer to the hospital the picture of a comfortable morning nap, but not strong enough to interfere further in the realization of the wish to lie abed. The dream is a compromise between two wishes, and that is why it is somewhat absurd. Thus we have a clew to the reason for nonsensical dreams; and for Freud it has been, as generally, the apparent obstacles which have shed the most light. For here we begin to see into the mechanism of character.

The incoherent quality comes from the compromise, in which, because two or more wishes interfere, none is fully satisfied: each wish is in fact, as language aptly has it, 'compromised.' The same mechanism is often evident in daily life, as when with a great show of pity someone dwells fondly and repetitiously on the imperfections of another. Here the wish to detract from another person is modified by the wish to live up to convention. The pity is not genuine, because, as the person's conduct shows, it is not strong enough to override the propensity to aspersion. The result is hypocritical and absurd, and in many cases goes so far as to be unintelligible. I have been present when a man literally tortured his wife on a quiet moonlight evening by ostentatiously reiterating, with minor variations, for two hours the sedulous query—" Darling, are you perfectly comfortable? Are you sure you don't need more wraps? " The underlying motive (as I knew from other sources) was torture, but whatever merciful impulses the husband had were so fully expressed in the *form* of his solicitations, that the hints and protestations made to him by others present and by his wife availed nothing. The husband enjoyed the evening immensely; but the friends were mystified and made uncomfortable, and one remarked afterwards, " He must be crazy! " In dreams such confounding of motive often goes so far that the dream is, notoriously, unintelligible. The most nonsensical of them are complicated by many wishes, and these

THE DOCTRINE OF THE 'WISH'

often of a deeply suppressed order; so that it is a long task to unravel them. Nor can the result be always described in a few pages. I will give one of the simpler cases of an apparently meaningless dream.*

A girl of about seventeen once asked me to explain this dream. "I met a certain older woman of my acquaintance, on the street. She put out her hand to shake hands with me. I was about to do the same when all my teeth fell out and into my hand."

"Well," I said, "you clearly do not like this older woman. Why not?"

"No, I don't like her," said she, and paused so irresolutely that I repeated my "Why?"

"Well, I suppose it is because she likes a certain young girl of my own age and always tries to come in between us and keep us apart. This girl is my dearest friend."

"And with which of these is the thought of teeth connected?"

---

* Freud's "Traumdeutung" gives many complicated dream-analyses (Deuticke, Leipzig and Vienna, 3d edition, 1911). The English translation by A. A. Brill is entitled "The Interpretation of Dreams" (Allen & Macmillan, London and New York, 1913).

"I have no idea," said the girl, pausing again. Then she added, coloring slightly, "The only thing I recall is that this older woman when she kisses my friend, as she often does, will nibble her cheek playfully like a mother-cat pretending to bite her kitten. And I hate to see her do it."

With this the dream was of course cleared up; it was the polite and blameless equivalent of saying to the older woman when encountering her on the street, "I would rather lose my teeth than greet you affectionately" (nibble):—a version of the matter which brought a sudden gleam of intelligence to the face of the girl who had had the dream. It is not often that a nonsensical dream is so easily interpreted; yet even here, as the reader sees, the wishes or motives involved have their roots in the very depths of character. The rôle played by the teeth is interesting because it is halfway symbolic; that is, while the teeth serve as a symbol of repugnance, their associated context in the dreamer's mind shows clearly how they come to have such a meaning.* Symbolism is very common in dreams, but it is often excessively obscure.

* In hysteria, vomiting is regularly a symptom of repugnance, not of indigestion.

THE DOCTRINE OF THE 'WISH' 11

A further class of dreams, those of anguish and of horror, seem less amenable to the Freudian explanation. These are frequently dreams of the death of a near relative or friend, in which the dreamer experiences an agony of sorrow (or remorse). Thus Freud relates: * "One day I find a lady very downcast and tearful. She says, 'I don't want to see my relatives ever again; they must abominate me.' Then she relates, almost in the same breath, that she is put in mind of a dream (the significance of which she of course does not know) which she had when she was four years old; and it runs as follows—' A lynx or a fox is walking along the roof, and then something falls down or I fall down, and they bring my mother out of the house dead.' Hereupon she weeps bitterly. I had hardly told her that this dream must signify that in her childhood she wished to see her mother dead, and that it is because of this dream that she imagines that her relatives detest her, when she brings out a bit of further evidence to explain the dream: she was once, as a very young child, plagued by a street-urchin who called her 'Lynx-Eye'; and when she was three years old a tile from the

* *Op. citat.*, S. 187.

roof had fallen on her mother's head and cut it so that it bled."

Freud's recognition of the existence of such morbid wishes has offended some persons, who pretend, I suppose, that human nature is not capable of anything so unlovely. Yet I am sure that no one has had to do with children without hearing all too frequently—" You mean old thing! I hope you die! So there now!"—and this uttered with all childish vehemence. In fact, this is perhaps the earliest and most typical reaction of a child when it is vexed by other, and especially by older, persons; a situation that it does not know how to cope with otherwise. The most trifling irritation will often provoke it. But the child evidently finds that the wish is futile and suppresses it, having hit on more effective means for overriding opposition. Yet if with years of discretion the motives that suppress such a wish become strong, it must not be forgotten that the circumstances which tend to keep it alive and active may grow in gravity and in urgency. The young woman who keeps her fiancé waiting for forty years while she ministers to a crippled parent has an indefeasible interest in the timely decease of her burden. And

THE DOCTRINE OF THE 'WISH'

certainly there is no clergyman but has often witnessed at funerals how the chastening hand of bereavement is borne with a sprightliness and cheer, not to say alacrity, that have their roots elsewhere than in fortitude and faith.

So in the instance just cited from Freud, if a woman feels that she is detested by her relatives and if she never wishes to see them again, there are two ways of escape—she can go, *or they* can go! The dream of her childhood envisaged the second and more delectable alternative; and when later in life she found herself in a similar quandary the memory of this dream persistently suggested itself to her more innocent self. This is the mechanism of 'temptation.' But if such a consummation was 'wished,' why even in the dream should it be contemplated with anguish? Freud's answer is that while this was wished, other wishes also comprised in the character wished the opposite. For many other reasons, and these the less selfish ones, the woman by no means wished to see her relatives demise. These more rational wishes, which in ordinary waking hours are strong enough to hold the morbid wish in abeyance, constitute the individual's recognized character. It is they, or the mechanisms that embody them, which need the recuperation of sleep; it is they which 'go to sleep.' Whereupon the wishes which have been held in idleness, and are therefore not fagged, are able to exercise themselves in opposition to the upper group. But sleep is partial and of varying degrees, and a dream so contrary to the person's habitual and normal attitude cannot be put through without arousing the upper group, which then reacts with just the same emotions that it would have in face of the actual waking contemplation of the unlovely wish executed. As is well known, the upper group is often completely aroused by such a dream, and the dreamer finds himself wide-awake and under strong emotional strain. Freud calls this upper group of wishes, which is always the prevailing character of the individual, the 'censor.' Thus a person who has suppressed wishes, and very few have not, has the rudiments of double, or indeed of multiple, personality—a thing which in practical morals has often been shrewdly noted. In fact, Freud has amply demonstrated that 'possession by devils' is not a merely literary figure of the New Testament.

To the question, then, whether a person 'wishes

THE DOCTRINE OF THE 'WISH' 15

to have a painful dream,' Freud's answer is, of course, No. But the submerged part of a personality contains many wishes which the better portion ordinarily holds in check, but which, if they succeed in realizing themselves even in a dream, arouse the upper personality to feelings of horror and remorse. This view, so far from being novel or subversive, fits at once into the picture which the most ancient moralists have given us. A fearful dream is an exact counterpart on the plane of imagination, of what only too often happens in actual waking life: a person's lower self 'gets the better of him,' he commits an evil deed, instantly 'comes to himself' again, and suffers an agony of remorse. Unmistakably one of his selves wished the evil and did it, while another self surveys the result with consternation. Again the same thing happens in revery, where the upper self (censor) is somewhat relaxing its vigilance: many a man in revery contemplates deeds and projects which he would not let himself carry out, or even think of, in moments of complete alertness. But such revery is an instructive indulgence, for it is a perfectly just psychological observation that, "As a man thinketh in his heart, so is he." It might also be called Freud's motto. The suppressed motives gain currency if thus exercised, and by just so much are amalgamated with the upper self and become a part of it. The 'still small voice' is the popular but just designation for the protest of the semi-dormant upper self when, in revery, fancy, or imagination, lower impulses have succeeded in intruding on the field of consciousness; and I know of no more cardinal doctrine for the cultivation of moral character than that of the still small voice. But of this later. Our point here is that the sole difference between dreams, revery, and waking life is in the *degree* of vigilance exercised by the censor. In dreams the censor is most relaxed, and evil wishes which at no other time would be tolerated can then express themselves. If there are any! The dreams that a person has are significant of what does lie smoldering within him.

Such, in outline, is Freud's explanation of dreams. He has devised a method, 'psychoanalysis,' for deciphering the more obscure ones. And, although many dreams are very refractory, and Freud himself looks on some of his analyses as incomplete or even doubtful, yet the results are so illuminating, and so comparable with phenomena

THE DOCTRINE OF THE 'WISH'

of the waking life, that I think no one who goes into the facts and scans them without bias will doubt the fundamental soundness of Freud's view that dreams are the work of wishes.

Now suppressed wishes find other means of expression than dreams, and means by which to influence the consciousness and acts of waking life. These are most startlingly evident in mental derangements, and it was in connection with hysteria and other nervous disorders that Freud commenced his study of human character. Into this field we need not go, although it is well to keep in mind that no sharp line divides the normal from the abnormal, and that what Freud says of the normal mechanism is well substantiated by careful observation of the exaggerated abnormal cases.

Another phenomenon which shows the working of subterranean forces in character is that of wit and humor. After reviewing the long list of theories and definitions of humor, which is as dense a jungle of misconception as anywhere exists, Freud caps them all with his simple formula that every form of wit or humor is nothing but a means of 'letting the cat out of the bag.' * But what

* "Der Witz" (Leipzig and Wien, 2d edition, 1912).

cat, what bag, and what are the means? The cat is one of these suppressed wishes, the bag is the confinement imposed by the vigilant censor, and the means are a variety of devices to trick the censor, particularly by taking advantage of the latter's weak points. Thus the man who said, "The Rev. Mr. — 's prayer yesterday was the most eloquent prayer that has ever been presented before a Boston audience," was really charging the preacher with caring more about his audience than about God. But it eludes the speaker's censor because, firstly, the remark barely misses of conveying high praise; secondly, because the same or similar phrase with 'sermon' put in the place of 'prayer' is fairly habitual and not a few persons are able to rattle the remark off 'without thinking.' For precisely the same reasons it can be counted on to pass the censor of anyone to whom it is addressed. In fact, while such a comment is as derogatory as it can well be, it is so nicely adjusted to the weaknesses of the average person's censor that probably even the preacher who was its victim would have been unable to take serious offense. Thus this sly tribute of praise gives vent to the teller's suppressed attitude of hatred (or it may be envy,

THE DOCTRINE OF THE 'WISH'

etc.) without traversing any of the accepted social conventions. And the censor is generally strong on conventions.

And, further, it clears the way for a similar release of suppressed wish in the person to whom the comment is made. The function of a joke in the inventor's mind and its rôle in the minds of those who hear or read it are not always identical. As to the former, of course, humor occurs spontaneously or not at all: one cannot grind out wit to order. At the most one can cultivate a facetious habit of mind, which means a censor that rigidly regards the conventions but imposes no more sincere check on illicit wishes. One can see this in many degrees, and one recalls that the ' saint ' is traditionally grave and shows no trace of facetiousness. Wit is never saintly, and is always sly; yet, as will appear, it need not be vicious. But to rack one's brains for a joke is to court the impossible. When a joke comes, it infallibly produces a smile even though the person be quite alone. I think there can be no doubt, although here I am going exactly counter to Freud,* that this is due to an

* Freud, strangely enough as I think, refers the smile or laugh to energy coming from the censor and due to the latter's relaxing its hold on the suppressed wish.

overflow of energy from the hitherto suppressed wish into the facial muscles; why just these muscles is not known, although one gets a hint from Darwin's book on "The Expression of the Emotions in Man and Animals." After this, if the suppressed wish is sufficiently relieved by the one discharge, the joke is forgotten and the smile fades; but if the wish has a larger store of pent-up energy, the joke lingers in the mind and the smile on the face; it may be for days. A person who is habitually in this condition is, in the vernacular, a 'chucklehead.' But, on the other hand, the censor may be aroused to greater vigilance; and the person 'straightens out his face' and 'sobers down.' Just what shall happen depends on the relative strengths of the suppressed wish and of the censor, and on the amount of release which the joke affords as well as on the degree of violence which it does to the censor. A really 'slick' piece of wit, like Mark Twain's "When in doubt, tell the truth," does no violence to anyone's censor, and is a perennial outlet for one's contempt of deceitful humanity. It is sly but not vicious. Freud here involves us in a doctrine of the 'latent energy of suppressed wishes'; and although this may sound

THE DOCTRINE OF THE 'WISH' 21

highly metaphorical, it is an exact statement and easily explained in the strictest physiological terms.*

The reception of a piece of humor by a second person is subject to the same principles, but the conditions present more chance for variation. In the first place, the recipient may not have any suppression such as the joke would release. At a dinner-table where the hostess was a Christian Scientist I once heard a professional diner-out relate how, in a Christian Scientist's family of his acquaintance, the pet cat had given birth to blind kittens. It was very sad. The 'Science' healer was immediately consulted, and after ten days of absent treatment the kittens were restored to perfect sight. I tried in vain to kick the gentleman under the table as soon as I scented his drift, but he was not to be deterred; the joke was a frost; and after he departed the house rang with injurious comment:—he was a 'wife-beater,' and she, poor thing, might even then be 'committing suicide.' †

* Cf. the Supplement, "Response and Cognition."
† And you, O Gentle Reader (to use an outworn mode), I fear may like this tale because it grants you three suppressed wishes—a dig at Christian Science, one at the venom of indignant hostesses, and a vision of the discomfiture of

It is clear enough that a piece of humor will miss fire when fired at a person who has not the requisite suppressed complex. In the instance just given this second person had not only no such suppression but the very reverse, and the joke was taken for exactly what it was—an act of aggression against Christian Science. Clearly, then, humor can generally be passed only among persons of similar suppressions ('prejudices'); and one notes, in fact, that it flows freely in circles of intimate friends, while it gives place to stiff formality in other assemblies in proportion to the lack of an established congeniality. The man who wants to be witty before a large audience must limit himself to ventilating suppressions which are fairly common to the race. The safest way is to appeal to the Old Adam in us all which secretly regards the fellow-man as a rival and prospective antagonist. The Germans aptly name this principle '*Schadenfreude*,' for which we seem to have no equivalent. Even here the censors are of different degrees of strictness, and one must adapt one's *Schadenfreude*

that ubiquitous nuisance, the professional funny-man. Yes, and a fourth, for it shows me foolishly trying to avert impending gloom by kicking vainly against the unfeeling air.

THE DOCTRINE OF THE 'WISH'   23

to the average censor of the audience. One person finds it excruciatingly funny to hear a wan and lonely old woman sitting down on a tack; while another can scarcely bear to hear that Mr. X., the once promising but now middle-aged and disappointed senator, "has a glorious future behind him."

During the administration of one of our recent Presidents, the following varieties of unfriendly comment could be heard in different levels of society:

"That 'ere Rosyvelt is a —— —— crazy fool" (corresponding to no censor at all).

"The Old Colonel acts like a brainless bedlamite" (where the reference to a time of extreme popularity, the charm of alliteration, the indirectness of ' acts *like*,' and the somewhat cryptic value of the word 'bedlamite' all conspire to beguile a feeble censor).

"Ah, yes! Teddy is unquestionably our headforemost citizen" (affectionate playfulness of the form 'Teddy,' and approximation to the encomiastic 'foremost citizen').

"In the last great Day of Judgment President Roosevelt will undoubtedly take his place somewhere between St. George and St. Vitus."

Probably no one could be found to whom all four statements would be acceptable, although their actual purport is identical. On the other hand, the friends of Mr. Theodore Roosevelt and of his policies would not tolerate the first form, nor exactly relish the second or the third, while I have heard his warm admirers laugh heartily at the fourth.

It may be asked why, if this theory of wit is sound, a person should ever be brought to tolerate a joke at his own expense; since he surely harbors no suppressed wishes against himself. The answer could be given that there is in each of us, besides the self-asserting or egoistic instinct with its allied group of wishes, an 'instinct of self-abasement'; *
if this is the case, any wishes allied to this instinct, if suppressed (as they would be by an egoistic censor), would predispose a person to relish humor directed against himself. I have not observed a case which I feel to be certainly of this sort. But I know of two other types; one false and one genuine. There are persons quite devoid of humor who

* Cf. William McDougall: "Social Psychology" (Methuen, London. 8th edition, 1914, p. 62).

have learned to watch others and to laugh almost exactly when and as they laugh. One such, a woman, passes among her friends for a witty creature; she has gathered a large repertoire of witticisms from the most approved sources, along with the proper mimetic accompaniment. These she displays along with other allurements on social occasions. Since she has a tolerable memory and fair intelligence, she carries the thing off rather well. Sometimes, however, the machinery creaks; her fun is not always apposite, and at the jokes of others she is apt to laugh a hint too loudly in order to prove that she sees the point and, unfortunately, just a breath too late (at her own jewels she exhibits only a studied and discreet smile); if it is a joke which divides the assembly into amused and indignant factions, she is lost. Some find her very amusing; so do I. Now such a person, if confronted by a joke at his or her own expense, and if something in the context gives him the clew that it is a joke, has to decide again from the context whether to be angry or to feign amusement. If the occasion as a whole has been intimate and friendly the person will often decide to emit gales of laughter.

The other sort of case is where the aspect which is pointed out for ridicule is so little intrinsic to the person's actual self that this actual self is quite able to experience *Schadenfreude* over it; he 'objectifies' it. Once in camp I was trying to chop wood, while another, more experienced chap looked on. I was doing it abominably, and at one stroke that was worse even than the others I said, to save my face, I suppose, " Oh, dear, I missed that stroke." " *Which* one? " said he dryly; and set me to laughing till the tears ran down my cheeks. Since then I have learned to chop wood, and I should now feel annoyed if an onlooker were to ask me which of my strokes I referred to as the unsuccessful one. When grown-ups assemble for a frolic and play children's games, they laugh as heartily and as genuinely at their own awkwardness and failures as at those of others. A man or woman not doing so betrays the fact that he or she is not sufficiently mature to have left the petty prowesses of childhood behind; but still accounts them an adornment of personality and a matter for pride. This in an adult is 'arrested development.'

One further point about wit. The man to whom a joke spontaneously occurs usually merely smiles, though he sometimes laughs; while the man to whom the joke is narrated usually laughs, though he may merely smile. This difference is due to the incubation process in the former case, where the suppressed wish is working against opposition, and by the time it gets to the surface it has not so much energy left to flow over into the facial muscles. In the man to whom a joke is told the suppressed wish is released *suddenly* and without effort on its own part, so that its whole energy passes into the laugh. Apart from this factor the phenomenon depends solely on the relative strengths of wish and censor.

Such, in brief, is Freud's doctrine of wit. The mechanism is the same as that which produces dreams, the only difference being that since in the latter case the censor is partially in abeyance, the wishes which can then manifest themselves are of a sort so profoundly suppressed that they could hardly pass the waking censor, even in the form of wit. They are of things too deep for jesting; as in the case narrated of little 'Lynx-Eye.' They are indeed usually quite unknown to the waking consciousness, so that there is no more effectual means for exploring the hidden depths of one's own character than the careful interpretation of one's own dreams. Here, too, the censor may be sufficiently alert to require the seditious impulse to assume a highly disguised form; as in the case of wit. On the other hand, all such suppressions as can come out in wit are just so much the freer to express themselves during sleep; and they do so with the greater license, as may be seen by a comparison of obscene jokes with obscene dreams. Both wit and dreams reveal the deeper levels of character, and Freud is entitled to say: Tell me what a man laughs at and dreams about, and I will tell you what man he is.

It is not alone in these two classes of phenomena that suppressed wishes come into evidence. They manifest themselves, as some of the foregoing illustrations have intimated, in every act of daily life. And this is the more important fact for our present aim, for it shows us 'wishes' or, better, purposes so little suppressed that we can observe them actually operating to guide or misguide the conduct hour by hour of any human being. And here we begin to see that character is nothing but an assemblage of purposes, and that the question for ethics is—What shall the purposes be?—and,

How shall they be organized? But I must not anticipate.

Freud, whose professional interest is medical, has written a fascinating book, called in English "The Psychopathology of Everyday Life,"* and several shorter monographs on the less conspicuous manifestations of wish interaction. These, with several able works that they have inspired,† establish a new art of reading character and enable us for the first time to study the subject intelligently. Here, as always with a new source of insight, such knowledge as we previously had of character is not subverted, but amplified and made more precise. We have always to some extent read one another's character without knowing quite how; the novelist, the dramatist, and the actor have undertaken to depict it. I believe it is not too much to say that now for the first time we know what character is.

In the ordinary phenomena of everyday life the

* Berlin, 4th edition, 1912: English translation by A. A. Brill (Unwin, London, and Macmillan, New York, 1914.)

† Of these perhaps the most notable are the works of Dr. Ernest Jones. His "Papers on Psycho-Analysis" (Wm. Wood, New York, 1913) are the best single work in English from which to derive an understanding of the whole Freudian psychology.

subconscious motives are often not deeply suppressed; so little so, in fact, that it is more a question of their being for the moment in or out of 'attention.' Thus there are many varieties of handshake—the robust, the anemic, the cordial and sincere, the officially 'cordial' but actually indifferent, the disdainful, the hostile, the handshake of commerce (hard grip with eyes sedulously averted), etc., etc. We all 'instinctively' read this silent language, and profit by it; and the finer nuances are contained in small tensions and pressures that a third person often cannot see. Thus when at introduction a person grasps your hand with all apparent cordiality, and at the same time you feel it infinitesimally but firmly propelled away from himself, you know that the meaning is 'So far and no farther; and so far only for the sake of appearances.' The person doing this is often quite unaware of the slight pushing away of your hand, unaware of the little part-gesture that so belies the expression of his face; yet at another moment he is probably conscious enough of some sort of unfriendly feeling toward you. The person has lied with his face and with the general gesture of his hand, but in spite of himself the motive to be con-

THE DOCTRINE OF THE 'WISH'

cealed has significantly qualified his act. The fact is this: one cannot extend one's hand toward another with cordiality (i.e., to seize and to retain) when another motive within one is making for a different use of the same muscles. A close observer would undoubtedly detect equivocation in the facial expression as well. This hindrance besets every lie, whether white, black, or gray.

These motives which unconsciously shade and qualify all overt conduct, and which are not so deeply suppressed but that they can at another time come to consciousness and themselves determine the overt conduct, are called by Freud 'preconscious' ('*vorbewusst*'); and the distinction between conscious and preconscious includes the ordinary psychological distinction between the field of 'attention' and 'introspection' *and* the 'fringe of consciousness,' the subconscious, etc. From the preconscious there is every shade of gradation down to the deeply suppressed. Furthermore, preconscious motives, like conscious ones, are invariably reënforced by others which lie deeper and these by others still more deeply suppressed, and so on down. A few illustrations.

In treating of writing in his "Papers on

Psycho-Analysis," Dr. Ernest Jones describes how his typist, who has previously worked in a lawyer's office, is prone in copying his manuscripts to mistake his own words for legal terms more habitual to her; thus she will read and write down 'illegal' for '*illogical*,' etc. Dr. Jones adds (p. 71), "I have found that distinctness of calligraphy is powerless to prevent such mistakes." Why 'calligraphy'? thought I, since of course calligraphy is necessarily distinct, and Jones besides being a careful writer perfectly knows his classics. Of course he had unconsciously written 'calligraphy' instead of 'chirography,' because of the delicate boast which is thus conveyed that his handwriting is always, even when indistinct, 'beautiful.' To this extent his ego-complex had eluded his censor. This was too good to lose, so at the bottom of the page I wrote in pencil, with reference to 'calligraphy' above, "Should be 'chiro-': Another case of *Verschreiben* [*lapsus calami*] w. odious cause." And then the joke was on me. I had fully intended to write 'obvious,' and was as astonished to see 'odious' as if another person had written it. And another had—my own suppressed other which had been egregiously condemning Dr. Jones's far less blameworthy slip of the pen. Not every page of print records thus three slips; but they are frequent and almost invariably symptomatic. To show the continuity of these suppression phenomena, it should be noted here that my 'odious' for 'obvious' will by another person be accounted a 'mere slip of the pen,' 'pure accident' ('like nonsensical dreams'), a 'joke' on me, a significant symptom about me, or a hateful piece of 'spite'—according to the motives in that other person's mind and their relative strength.

It is well known that an author cannot read his own proof so well as another person can who is less tempted to preoccupation with the contents; and many persons read their own proofs twice, once for the thought and again for the spelling, etc.; because each set of considerations suppresses for the time being the other. But habit and other preconscious motives exercise specific influence as well. For the first few times of my seeing the words 'Cort Theatre' I read them 'Court Theatre.' Dr. Jones, an Englishman, relates how on searching an American newspaper for English political news, his attention was caught by the heading 'General Danger'; on looking more closely he saw that it was 'German Danger.' Where one word has two meanings, the wrong meaning is often 'read in.' Once after the second of a series of three subscription dances, I sent to the person in charge (a university professor) to obtain two extra tickets for 'the last dance.' He wrote me back, "The 'last' dance has occurred. You probably mean the next." But so eager had he been to make me out a fool that he inclosed no tickets, and I had to write again to assure him that it was not to a dance which had taken place that I was now planning to bring friends. At that time I had never heard of Freud and was utterly mystified by such 'unaccountable stupidity.' Undoubtedly the man 'apperceived' my letter as a plain request for tickets to 'last week's dance'; and this trick his preconscious egoism played on him.

In reading aloud, slips of the tongue are in the same way symptomatic, and it is well known how one's inner attitude toward the theme alters one's word-emphasis; it is practically impossible for anyone except a professional actor to read with feeling and 'expression' a composition with which one is not in sympathy. Nor is the actor's ability to do so a matter of habit and training; the

THE DOCTRINE OF THE 'WISH' 35

mimetic professions attract a peculiar type of person—far below the average in steadfastness of character (settled convictions, point of view, etc.), and this lack compensated by an abnormal development of egoism. Having little or no *fixed* character of his own, the actor is by virtue of this very defect able to fall into any rôle that is handed him ready-made; he has no deeply ingrained wishes, suppressed or other, which work against his 'part.' He can be all things to all men; while his ego-complex is always gratified (however disgraceful the rôle) by the glamour of protagonism.* A man or woman with positive character is disqualified for being an all-round actor, and will succeed only if he or she sticks to a certain 'line' of 'congenial' rôles; and what this 'line' shall be is determined by both his conscious and subconscious wishes. The fact accounts for certain peculiarities of dramatic professional life.

In view of the only too obvious and universally acknowledged fact that a man's general trend of

* My first hint of this was from a shrewdly observed short story of, I believe, Alphonse Daudet's. Since then I have seen at first hand ample confirmation of the point. Out of his 'part' the actor is not infrequently a downright imbecile, and a monster of egoism. The actor's is merely the excessively mercurial and labile character.

conversation, like his deeds, expresses his character, it is amusing to see with what incredulity persons will often receive the statement that the finer details of speech and action (such as 'slips of the tongue' and the previously mentioned 'slips of the pen') are significant as well. A man once even argued with me that the manner of a handshake possessed no significance. And *lapsus linguæ* are often accounted one of the pet absurdities of the Freudians. Once in going to make a call on Mrs. A. I had to pass the house of Mrs. B., who was sitting on her front verandah. I am always irritated by Mrs. B. and at this time was feeling particularly out of patience with her because she had not shown herself very neighborly during a recent illness of Mrs. A. But I like Mr. B. immensely and wish to 'keep in' with the family; so that I had to nibble Mrs. B.'s bait and spend an impatient half-hour on her verandah. When I arose to go I undertook to be amiably untruthful and to say, "I'm so glad that you were out on the verandah as I was going by." But my treacherous lips actually brought out, "I'm so sorry that you were," etc. The reader may be skeptical as to the cause of this slip; but Mrs. B.

was not, and did not invite me to her house for over a year; as served me quite right.

The skepticism of many persons in regard to the symptomatic quality of these little lapses is in itself an interesting phenomenon. Firstly, I detect in myself a reluctance to urging the point:—the other man wags his head and chuckles so patronizingly, "Oh, you Freudians are all daft." I almost burst with suppressed merriment, for, having done my duty in offering a valuable secret, the secret is still mine: my censor is disarmed because I have done my best and been mocked; and so *Schadenfreude* is let loose. I am little disposed to press the matter. An aged rustic at a circus gazed long and uncomprehendingly at the cassowary and after a time exclaimed aloud, " Gosh dern it all; ther' ain't no sech bird!" The cassowary, it is said, continued to smile, and was not moved to argue the point.

Secondly, the skeptical are often made so by a suppressed wish. Apart from the common reluctance in persons to accept a truth frankly which they see is so simple that they ought to have found it out for themselves, many persons have the dim but instantaneous intuition that if the little nuances of conduct *are* symptomatic, their own lives must be one long self-betrayal. Therefore this must not and shall not be true; they *will* not believe it. Against such a disconcerting discovery the (partly suppressed) ego defends itself and obscures the man's 'critical' judgment. I once met a fairly well educated business man who thus passionately rejected everything pertaining to Freud. The man was himself one of the most unconscionable liars who ever lived; he distorted every fact to his own liking, and so grossly that few persons were misled except (in the end) himself. *He* came to be gravely self-deluded, and his life was one long unconscious self-exposure. This man could see nothing but nonsense in Freud. Early in life he had calculated, as so many do, that a lie is best couched in the form of a 'reluctant admission,' as thus: "I cannot any longer resist the conviction that So-and-so is a complete failure in business." (From which you could safely infer that So-and-so was a successful and hated rival of this man.) This euphemistic precaution finally crystallized into the set phrase, "I confess frankly that," etc., which finally was observed by the man's acquaintances (non-Freudians) so invariably to lead up to an

THE DOCTRINE OF THE 'WISH' 39

amazing whopper that they in turn fell into a habit. In talking to one another, if one of them caught himself stretching the truth, he would correct himself merely by playfully adding, "I confess it frankly." The man in question had alleged that he had 'never dreamed,' but one evening when dreams were the topic of conversation, and a person seemed to be 'out of it' who had never had any dreams, he proceeded to narrate some of his own (the persons present were comparative strangers and might be expected not to know of his interesting idiosyncrasy) until a Freudian present was moved to a point of honor, and exclaimed, "I beg your pardon, Sir, but since you are not a Freudian, you are unwittingly making the most intimate revelations. I do not wish to be an eavesdropper, even in such a way." This abandoned person, whose motto had become literally, "Evil be thou my good," exhibited later in life, it was said, an almost pitiful emotional recoil at any mention of deceit and untruth, and at one time was known to say, "The word 'lie' is not in my lexicon." It scarcely needed to be.

Illustrations of the influence of more or less suppressed 'wishes' on all phases of life could be multiplied without number; for in fact life itself *is* nothing but these wishes working themselves out in action. Some of them are 'conscious,' others 'preconscious,' while others are hidden more deeply in the once mysterious levels of the subconscious. The reader who cares to follow this aspect of our subject further will find a great store of examples in the volume by Dr. Jones to which I have already referred, and in the works of Freud himself. I will narrate but one further case, because it is unlike any which I have found recorded and shows an even subtler working of the unconscious than is sometimes met with. I was present at the incident to be related, and will vouch for the accuracy of the account. Some of the 'wishes' involved are of the sort that more nearly resemble 'subconscious ideas.'

On a day in July, five men, M., L., H., and two others, all intimate friends, spent the afternoon at a country-club playing golf. A sixth man, T., an intimate friend of all except of H., with whom he was merely acquainted, was to dine with the party on the verandah of the club-house. T. arrived late and found the five friends seated at table and his own place waiting for him. In the course of the

THE DOCTRINE OF THE 'WISH'   41

evening, conversation fell on a certain Miss Z., a distant cousin of T.'s, and a person with whom all six of the men were more or less acquainted. Miss Z. was an attractive young woman who had taken a doctorate of philosophy, and written a book or two on esthetics; she had recently become engaged to a young architect, a specialist in concrete construction, and was to be married in the following month. M., L., H., T., and probably the other two, knew these items. When Miss Z. was mentioned, L. turned to H. and said, "Tell T. [her cousin] what you said this afternoon about Miss Z.'s engagement." H. turned this off lightly, and went on to something else; whereupon L. said again, "Oh, go ahead! Tell T. what you said." H. evaded the point once more, and undertook to change the subject. Then T., whose curiosity was now aroused, broke in, "Oh, come on, H.! What was it about Miss Z.'s engagement?" H. again parried.

At this so marked reluctance on the part of H. to repeat his remark about Miss Z. and her engagement, T. (her cousin) began to suspect that the speech had been in some way derogatory to Miss Z. This exasperated T., who, for an intelligible but not a very good reason, already slightly disliked H. Then T., who had only just arrived on the scene and had no knowledge of the speech which H. refused to repeat, broke out with considerable heat and made the apparently idiotic declaration:—. "*Well, if you won't tell it, I will!*" H. still refused, and T. then brought out from no visible source: "Well, what you said was that Miss Z. is going to exchange the abstract for the concrete!"

This was in fact exactly what H. had said in the afternoon, and what L. had tried to get him to repeat. As all the persons present knew that T. had had no opportunity of learning what the remark had been, their astonishment amounted to consternation. The most astonished person of all was T. himself; while H. was silent and a trifle sullen, as if he half suspected that a trick had been played on him.

This incident more nearly resembles 'thought-transference' than any other that I have witnessed; and I happen to know positively that T. was in no way apprised of H.'s remark before he, T., reproduced it. Nevertheless the explanation is simple. The little word-play on which the incident turns is derived by a simple process from

THE DOCTRINE OF THE 'WISH' 43

very simple data—Miss Z.'s quality of *femme-savante*, and her *fiancé's* of concrete builder. It occurred ' spontaneously ' to the minds of both H. and T. This is in itself no more remarkable than the case of two acquaintances meeting on a cloudy morning, and saying simultaneously, each with a glance at the other's umbrella, " Ah, I see that you are expecting rain." In our case the observation passed the incubation process in H.'s mind in the afternoon, and was consciously spoken by him to his friends. In T.'s mind it was still in the incubation and had never come to consciousness, for T. so affirms, and says further that until the words came out of his mouth he had no idea as to what he was going to say, to back up his rash challenge to H. This shows that the speech was passed through its last stages of incubation and brought to utterance by the stimulus of the peculiar social situation; especially by the slight vexation felt toward H. That the speech should have come out without conscious foreknowledge of what it was to be is perfectly natural; if one comes to think of it, most of our talk is uttered in this way.

The two most interesting questions involved are: why H. had refused to repeat his so innocent remark of the afternoon, and why T. was prompted to risk a challenge which, since he was not *conscious* of anything wherewith to back it up, was practically certain to put him in a silly predicament. As to the former, it is safe to conjecture that H. secretly disliked T. perhaps even more than T. disliked H., and that when called on by L. to repeat himself for the benefit of T., had slightly the feeling of being ' put through his paces,' being shown off to please T. This he would certainly resist; particularly as the joke to be repeated was now stale for four persons there present whom he did like. This feeling, that one's dignity is being invaded, is very deeply rooted, and one has often seen dogs, cats, and babies absolutely refuse to exhibit their little tricks and accomplishments when commanded to do so before a stranger; in such cases I, if I am the stranger, turn my back and the trick is instantly performed.

Secondly, as to T.'s foolish challenge. The evidence itself shows that T. did not know ' consciously ' what he expected to say further, for had he known he would almost certainly have expressed his irritation by saying: *not*, " Well, if you won't tell it, I will!" but, " You needn't trouble yourself to repeat your silly joke; it was only that Miss Z. is going to exchange the abstract for the concrete." The speech actually made sounds very much like the small boy's challenge to some slightly bigger tormentor, "If you don't gim'me back my jackknife, I'll, I'll, I'll——" Both speeches express anger, but in that of T. the note of impotence is replaced by one of foolhardiness. This is evidence, I think, that T.'s subconsciousness held in readiness not merely the play on 'abstract'-'concrete,' but a more or less comprehensive plan of action ('wish') with regard to the situation as a whole: T.'s upper consciousness could go on ranting as rashly as it liked, for T.'s subconsciousness had guessed the answer to the conundrum, and was pretty confident of its being the correct answer: it would produce it when wanted. As it did. This would be a very simple achievement for the subconsciousness, in comparison with the remarkable cases observed by Dr. Morton Prince in "Miss Beecham" and other of his patients.*

This completes our analysis. The case is merely an instance of the interplay between wishes and

* "The Dissociation of a Personality" (Longmans, Green, London, 1906). "The Unconscious" (Macmillan, New York, 1914).

ideas, partly conscious and partly subconscious, taking place under peculiarly dramatic circumtances. It would easily have converted a too-superficial observer to a firm belief in 'thought-transference'; and no one could have allayed this by suggesting that the case was possibly referable to 'muscle-reading,' for it quite certainly was not. It only remains to add that T. does not recall having uttered so foolish a challenge on any other occasion; and that, as Freudians will already have anticipated, H. professes at the present time to have not the slightest recollection of the episode, save that there was a dinner at the country-club at which So-and-so and So-and-so were present. And lastly, the identical jest about Miss Z.'s exchanging the abstract for the concrete turned up about a week later from a third and unquestionably independent source.

CHAPTER II

THE PHYSIOLOGY OF WISHES; AND THEIR INTEGRATION

THE foregoing pages will have sufficiently illustrated, I trust, what Freud means by his very comprehensive term 'wish.' I have dwelt on it at great length, because it is this 'wish' which transforms the principal doctrines of psychology and recasts the science; much as the 'atomic theory,' and later the 'ionic theory,' have reshaped earlier conceptions of chemistry. This so-called 'wish' becomes the unit of psychology, replacing the older unit commonly called 'sensation'; which latter, it is to be noted, was a *content* of consciousness unit, whereas the 'wish' is a more dynamic affair. In attempting to expound the change in psychology which is effected by this concept of the 'wish,' I shall have to go somewhat beyond anything which Freud himself has said or written, for he has mainly devoted himself to reshaping the science of psychiatry, *abnormal* psychology; and has not discussed at anything like so great length the general field of normal mind. But I shall try to limit myself to the *necessary implications* of his discoveries, in the field of normal psychology. And in doing this I am quite aware that the rank and file of psychologists to-day neither understand nor accept, if indeed they have ever dreamt of, these essential and, as I think, very illuminating implications. It shall be for the reader to judge whether the picture which emerges bears the stamp of truth.

Unquestionably the mind is somehow 'embodied' in the body. But how? Well, if the unit of mind and character is a 'wish,' it is easy enough to perceive how it is incorporated. It is, this 'wish,' something which the body as a piece of mechanism can *do:* a course of action with regard to the environment which the machinery of the body is capable of carrying out.* This capacity resides, clearly, in the parts of which the body consists

---

* Here the reader may raise the query—"Carry out without the directing influence of an intelligent soul?" To this I will ask the reader to accept provisionally the answer—Yes, *without*. But this merely because the question as raised, although familiar, is meaningless. We are not coming out to a psychology without a soul, unless by soul one means 'ghost-soul.' Quite on the contrary, Freud's is actually the first psychology *with* a soul.

and in the way in which these are put together; not so much in the matter of which the body is composed, as in the forms which this matter assumes when organized. If, now, the wishes *are* the soul, then we can understand in all literalness Aristotle's dictum, that the soul " is the *form* of a natural body endowed with the capacity of life "; soul is indeed the entelechy. Just as the spirit of any piece of machinery lies in what it can do, and this specific capacity lies in its plan and structure rather than in the brute matter through which this plan is tangibly realized, so precisely it is with the human spirit and the human body. The spirit and the matter of the body are two things: and in the case of machinery and engineering enterprises we can plan, alter, revise, estimate, purchase, and patent the spirit, before this is ever materially incorporated. Yet on the other hand, the spirit needs to be realized in a tangible body before it can effectively operate. In living human beings, certainly, the spirit *is* embodied.

In order to look at this more closely we must go a bit down the evolutionary series to the fields of biology and physiology. Here we find much talk of nerves and muscles, sense-organs, reflex arcs, stimulation, and muscular response, and we feel that somehow these things do not reach the core of the matter, and that they never can: that spirit is not nerve or muscle, and that intelligent conduct, to say nothing of conscious thought, can never be reduced to reflex arcs and the like; just as a printing-press is not merely wheels and rollers, and still less is it chunks of iron. If, then, we insist on there being a soul which nevertheless the biologist says that he cannot discover anywhere in the living tissues of the animal he studies, we are quite right. And the biologist has only himself to thank if he has overlooked a thing which lay directly under his nose. He has overlooked the *form of organization* of these his reflex arcs, has left out of account that step which assembles wheels and rollers into a printing-press, and that which organizes reflex arcs, as we shall presently see, into an intelligent conscious creature. Evolution took this important little step of organization ages ago, and thereby produced the rudimentary 'wish.'

It was a novelty. Yet so complete is the continuity of evolution, and when we watch it closely so little critical are the 'critical points' in any process, that we may overlook the advent of a genuine novelty howsoever important. Thus in geometry the step is infinitesimal between two parallel lines and two lines which meet in infinity,* yet the geometrical properties of the system are astoundingly different in the two cases. Now in the reflex arc a sense-organ is stimulated and the energy of stimulation is transformed into nervous energy, which then passes along an afferent nerve to the central nervous system, passes through this and out by an efferent or motor nerve to a muscle, where the energy is again transformed and the muscle contracts. Stimulation at one point of the animal organism produces contraction at another. The principles of irritability and of motility are involved, but all further study of *this* process will lead us only to the physics and chemistry of the energy transformations: will lead us, that is, in the direction of *analysis*. If, however, we inquire in what way such reflexes are combined or 'integrated' into more complicated processes, we shall be led in exactly the opposite direction, that of *synthesis*, and here we soon come, as is not sur-

* It is of course not true, though often said, that "parallel lines meet in infinity"; not true, that is, if parallel lines are "lines which are everywhere equally distant from each other."

prising, to a synthetic novelty. This is *specific response* or *behavior*. And the advent of specific response is a sufficiently critical point to merit detailed examination, since it is the birth of *awareness* and therewith of psychology itself.

In the single reflex something is done to a sense-organ and the process within the organ is comparable to the process in any unstable substance when foreign energy strikes it; it is strictly a chemical process; and so for the conducting nerve; likewise for the contracting muscle. It happens, as a physiological fact, that in this process stored energy is released, so that a reflex contraction is literally comparable to the firing of a pistol. But the reflex arc is not 'aware' of anything, and indeed there is nothing more to say about the process unless we should begin to analyze it. But even two such processes going on together in one organism are a very different matter. Two such processes require two sense-organs, two conduction paths, and two muscles: and since we are considering the result of the two in combination, the relative anatomical location of these six members is of importance. For simplicity I will take a hypothetical, but strictly possible, case. A small water-animal has

THE PHYSIOLOGY OF WISHES 53

an eye-spot located on each side of its anterior end; each spot is connected by a nerve with a vibratory silium or fin on the *opposite* side of the posterior end; the thrust exerted by each fin is toward the rear. If, now, light strikes one eye, say the right, the left fin is set in motion and the animal's body is set rotating toward the right like a rowboat with one oar. This is all that one such reflex arc could do for the animal. Since, however, there are now two, when the animal comes to be turned far enough toward the right so that some of the light strikes the second eye-spot (as will happen when the animal comes around facing the light), the second fin, on the right side, is set in motion, and the two together propel the animal forward in a straight line. The direction of this line will be that in which the animal lies when its two eyes receive equal amounts of light. In other words, by the combined operation of two reflexes the animal swims *toward the light*, while either reflex alone would only have set it spinning like a top. It now responds specifically in the direction of the light, whereas before it merely spun when lashed.

As thus described, this first dawn of behavior seems to present nothing so very novel; it is not more novel than the infinitesimal touch that makes two parallel lines meet somewhere off in infinity. The animal, it is true, is still merely 'lashed' into swimming toward the light. Suppose, now, that it possesses a *third* reflex arc—a 'heat-spot' so connected with the same or other fins that when stimulated by a certain intensity of heat it initiates a nervous impulse which stops the forward propulsion. The animal is still 'lashed,' but nevertheless no light can force it to swim " blindly to its death " by scalding. It has the rudiments of 'intelligence.' But so it had before. For as soon as two reflex arcs capacitate it mechanically to swim *toward light*, it was no longer exactly like a pinwheel: it could respond specifically toward at least one thing in its environment.

It is this objective reference of a process of release that is significant. The mere reflex does not refer to anything beyond itself: if it drives an organism in a certain direction, it is only as a rocket ignited at random shoots off in some direction, depending on how it happened to lie. But specific response is not merely in some random direction, it is *toward an object*, and if this object is moved, the responding organism changes its direction and still moves after it. And the objective reference is that the organism is *moving with reference to some object or fact of the environment*. In the pistol or the skyrocket the process released depends wholly on factors internal to the mechanism released; in the behaving organism the process depends partly on factors external to the mechanism. This is a difference of prime significance, for in the first case, if you wish to understand all about what the rocket is doing, you have only to look inside the rocket, at the powder exploding there, the size and shape of the compartment in which it is exploding, etc.; whereas, in order to understand what the organism is doing, you will just *miss* the essential point you look inside the organism. For the organism, while a very interesting mechanism in itself, is one whose movements turn on objects outside of itself, much as the orbit of the earth turns upon the sun; and these external, and sometimes very distant, objects are as much *constituents* of the behavior process as is the organism which does the turning. It is this *pivotal outer object*, the object of specific response, which seems to me to have been over-neglected.

The case cited, in which merely two reflex arcs enable an organism to respond specifically to the direction of a luminous object, is of course an extremely simple one. We have seen how much the addition of even a third reflex arc can contribute to the security of the animal as it navigates its environment, and to the apparent intelligence and 'purposiveness' of its movements. It is not surprising, then, that in animals as highly organized reflexly as are many of the invertebrates, even though they should possess no other principle of action than that of specific response, the various life-activities should present an appearance of considerable intelligence. And I believe that in fact this intelligence is solely the product of accumulated specific responses.* Our present point is that the specific response and the 'wish,' as Freud uses the term, are one and the same thing.

This thing, in its essential definition, is *a course of action which the living body executes or is prepared to execute with regard to some object or*

* The reader who is interested in the development of specific response into intelligence will enjoy the small volume of A. Bethe ("Dürfen wir den Ameisen und Bienen psychische Qualitäten zuschreiben?" Bonn, 1898), in which the author shows how the life-activities of ants and bees can be explained in terms of reflex process.

THE PHYSIOLOGY OF WISHES

some fact of its environment. From this form of statement it becomes clear, I think, that not only is this the very thing which we are generally most interested to discover about the lower animals— what they are doing or what they are going to do— but also that it is the most significant thing about human beings, ourselves not excepted. " Ye shall know them by their fruits," and not infrequently it is by one's own fruits that one comes to know oneself. It is true that the term ' wish ' is rather calculated to emphasize the distinction between a course of action actually carried out and one that is only entertained ' in thought.' But this distinction is really secondary. The essential thing for both animal behavior and Freud's psychology is the *course of action,* the purpose with regard to environment, whether or not the action is overtly carried out.

In this whole matter the introspective tradition, which has led psychology into so many unfruitful by-paths, is prepared to mislead us. We must go cautiously. In the first place, let us bear quite clearly in mind that in any living organism, human or animal, we have a very complicated mechanism in which the property of irritability is so united with the power of motion that in a purely mechanical way the organism becomes, on proper stimulation, an engine that behaves in a certain way *with reference to* a specific feature of its environment.* This is what we can safely conclude from merely watching the doings of any living creature. And we behold invariably that every living thing is in every waking moment doing something or other to some feature or other of its environment. It is going toward or away from something, it is digging or climbing, it is hunting or eating; more developed organisms are working or playing, reading, writing, or talking, are making money or spending it, are constructing or destroying something; and at a still higher stage of development we find them curing disease, alleviating poverty, comforting the oppressed, and promoting one or another sort of orderliness. All these cases are alike in this, that the individual is doing something definite to some part or other of its environment. In exact language its activity is a " constant function " of some feature of this environment, in just the same sense (although by a different mechan-

* I would not for a moment minimize the actuality of 'thought.' For the moment we are considering another aspect of the matter.

THE PHYSIOLOGY OF WISHES 59

ism) as the orbit of our earth is a constant function of the position of the sun around which it swings. This constant function, involving always the two things—living organism and environment —is that which constitutes behavior and is also precisely that which Freud has called, with a none too happy choice of term, the 'wish': as a glance at the illustrations given in Chapter I will show. And we must not forget that ' purpose,' in any sense you may choose howsoever intellectual or indeed moral, is precisely the same thing.

Now, in an organism which is about to perform overtly a course of action with regard to its environment, the internal mechanism is more or less completely set for this performance beforehand. The purpose about to be carried out is already embodied in what we call the ' motor attitude ' of the neuro-muscular apparatus; very much as a musical composition is embodied in a phonographic record. And this is why it is in some respects irrelevant whether the individual actually carries out its wish, or not. Something may intervene so that the mechanism is not finally touched off, the stimulus may not be quite strong enough on this occasion, etc.; but that the individual ever developed such a set of its mechanism is the important point. It will be touched off some day, and even if it is not, its presence cannot fail to react on other mechanisms, other motor attitudes. We blame a man who is prepared to tell a lie, nearly if not quite as much as one who actually tells one.

There is indeed excellent ground for believing that the one difference between thought and will is the difference between a motor attitude prepared and one that is touched off. In other words, the essential physiological condition for thought (whatever view one may otherwise hold as to the nature and place of consciousness) is the lambent interplay of motor attitudes, in which some *one* finally gains the ascendency, and goes over into overt conduct. This is no new doctrine, since it is just this which Spinoza had in mind when he declared that "The will and the intellect are one and the same." * Herbert Spencer gives us a somewhat closer view of this fact,† and modern psychology as a whole has begun to recognize it, as the remarkable tendency of otherwise divergent schools toward

* "Ethics." Part II, Prop. XLIX, Corol. See also the Scholium which follows.
† "The Principles of Psychology," 2d edition, Vol. I, Part IV, Chap. IX.

THE PHYSIOLOGY OF WISHES

some form of 'motor theory of consciousness' shows. Thus, too, William James writes: "Beliefs, in short, are rules for action; and the whole function of thinking is but one step in the production of active habits." * And all this is undoubtedly why it is true that as a man thinketh in his heart, so is he. For Freud these motor attitudes of the body, whether they emerge in overt behavior or not, are the will of the individual. And the development of character, in fact the whole drama of life, hinges on the development and reciprocal modification of motor settings, that is of purposes and wishes incorporated in the body. The manner of this interaction is our main theme, for it has a practical bearing on ethics.

Remarkably enough this reduces to an extremely simple principle which will be found to underlie anything which can be called behavior or conduct, from the silent bending of the sensitive tip of a plant's rootlet to the most subtly motivated act of man. Darwin describes, in his book on "The Power of Movement in Plants," † how the growing

---

* "The Varieties of Religious Experience." 1902, p. 444.
† New York, 1888, Chap. XII.

tip of a radicle is sensitive to gravity, moisture, and light, and when subject to one of these influences it transmits an impulse to an adjoining upper part of the rootlet which then bends in such a way that the tip is turned toward the center of the earth, or toward moisture or (in the third case) away from light. If all three forces are present at once, the tip is bent in that direction which provides the most moisture compatible with the greatest depth and the least light. Here we have a very simple case in which three reflexes combine to produce one movement which is a plain mechanical resultant of the movements which the three reflexes would have produced if each had acted alone. They combine because the three reflexes converge on the same motile tissue that bends the rootlet, and this contractile tissue obeys as well as it can the simultaneous commands of all three irritable centers. It is significant that Darwin concludes the volume with these words (p. 573): "It is hardly an exaggeration to say that the tip of the radicle thus endowed, and having the power of directing the movements of the adjoining parts, acts like the brain of one of the lower animals; the brain being seated within the anterior end of the body, receiving impressions from the sense-organs, and directing the several movements."

In the lower forms of animal life we find likewise that reflexes combine to diminish (interference) or to augment each other in the response. H. S. Jennings writes of infusorians,* that "under the simultaneous action of the two stimuli the infusorian may either react to the more effective of the two, whichever it is, without regard to the other, or its behavior may be a sort of compromise between the usual results of both." Of course in the former case the less effective stimulus is not without its effect, although this effect may be largely masked by the greater strength of the other factor. "If specimens showing the contact reaction [of settling down on solid objects] are heated, it is found that they do not react to the heat until a higher temperature has been reached than that necessary to cause a definite reaction in free swimming specimens. . . . On the other hand, both heat and cold interfere with this contact reaction. . . . Specimens in contact with a solid react less readily to chemicals than do free specimens, so that a

* "Behavior of the Lower Organisms." New York, 1906, pp. 92-3.

higher concentration is required to induce the avoiding reaction." In these ways the planarians are found to respond to specific temperatures, degrees of chemical concentration, and to specific *amounts of change* in the vital conditions which surround them. Always, stimuli which if given separately would produce the same response, augment each other when they are given simultaneously; while stimuli which separately would produce opposed responses, interfere with or cancel each other when given together.

In the case of such wonderful little creatures as bees we see the same principle extended. As we all know, one prominent part of the behavior of the worker bee is that it fares forth every warm morning, visits the flowers, and returns laden with honey to its hive; to its own hive and no other. It does this throughout the day. This is no simple mode of behavior, and we know that it rests on elaborate neuro-muscular mechanisms. The bee is guided by the characteristic odor of its hive, and of the flowers, by the visible appearance of its own hive and of the surroundings, and by that of the flowers which it selects to visit, by a sense of the sun's warmth, of the state of the atmosphere, of the

THE PHYSIOLOGY OF WISHES 65

downward pull of gravity (as it flies), perhaps by some not yet fully understood ' sense of direction,' and by many other sense-data. All these sensory impulses converging on the motor apparatus of the bee's legs, wings, and proboscis guide and impel it moment by moment through its daily rounds. There is no reason to believe, as so careful an observer as Bethe assures us, that any more mysterious (as, say, ' psychic ') factors than such plain sensori-motor reflexes are at any moment of the process involved. The fact is that just as in the case of our hypothetical little creature (p. 52), which by two reflex arcs was enabled to swim toward light and by a third was made to avoid too high a temperature (a very ' purposive ' response), so in the case of the bee several thousand reflex paths co-operating produce a behavior which both looks and is startlingly ' purposive.' The question arises at once, Is this purposiveness really the result of a merely mechanical interplay of reflex arcs, or has an invisible little ' soul ' already crept into the bee's ' pineal gland ' to direct operations? This we shall have to answer in no uncertain tone: the bee is a purely reflex creature. We have seen purposiveness arise from the mere presence in one organism of three reflex arcs, which cause an organism to seek light and to avoid being scalded; these are already two purposes.* In fact, as C. S. Sherrington has said, "In light of the Darwinian theory every reflex *must* be purposive." † And a combination of reflexes is even more markedly so. We have then no reason to doubt that Bethe is correct in saying of so complicated an organism as the bee, that all its (so highly purposive) activities are the work of integrated reflexes.

I have stated that the mechanical interaction of reflexes on one another reduces to a very simple principle, and before we consider reflex integration in vertebrates, it will be well to have this principle definitely in mind. The reciprocal influence of reflexes can be exerted, of course, only where they come together, and that is where they converge on a common motor-organ, or on a common efferent nerve leading out to the motor-organ. Now, as the physiologist Sherrington says,‡ "each receptor [sense-organ] stands in connection not

* "Yes, but not *conscious* purposes," I seem to hear the reader say. This is a point which I shall take up a little further on.

† "The Integrative Action of the Nervous System." New York, 1906, p. 235.

‡ *Op. citat.*, pp. 145-6.

THE PHYSIOLOGY OF WISHES 67

with one efferent only but with many—perhaps with all, though as to some of these only through synapses [nerve junctions] of high resistance." It is "approximately true" that "each final common path is in connection with practically each one of all the receptors of the body." This generalization is made of vertebrates, but it is fairly certain that a similar state of things holds throughout the animal and plant kingdoms (for plants, also, have sense-organs, nerves, and muscles). Now nature has not found it convenient to equip us with rotary means of locomotion, like the propeller of a ship; but has provided that every motion shall be made by the to-and-fro play of a member—fin, arm, or leg. Therefore the muscles exist in pairs, in each one of which one muscle moves the limb in a direction opposite to that in which the other muscle moves it; that is, the two muscles of a pair are antagonists. While the nervous impulse generated by any stimulus goes (or under certain circumstances can go) to any muscle of the body, the nervous paths are of different degrees of resistance, so that the main force of the impulse goes in certain few directions rather than in all. And one stimulus will effect somewhere a muscular contraction: some member of the body is moved. But many outer forces are simultaneously playing on the many sense-organs of the body, and they prompt the muscles to many different motions. Wherever these impulses converge to contract the same muscle, that muscle contracts with all the more force, and the limb moves. But when the sensory impulses run equally to the antagonistic muscles of a pair, the limb is naturally unable to move in opposite directions at the same time. If the two impulses are equal in amount the limb will not move at all. Such impulses cancel each other, and *do not contribute* to *behavior*. If we call the sum of all sense impulses at any moment the ' sensory pattern,' we shall practically always find that some portions of this pattern cancel themselves out by interference, in the way described, while the remaining portions augment one another and produce the individual's overt behavior and conduct. The impulses of the sensory pattern may be so weak as to produce no gross muscular contractions, but they will then cause varying degrees of muscular tonus; and this is that play of motor attitude which I have previously mentioned. It is thought. It differs from overt behavior only in the small degree of muscular

THE PHYSIOLOGY OF WISHES

action which it involves. The one fundamental principle is that no member can move in opposed directions at once, and impulses that impel to this efface each other. This is very simple: the complications to which it gives rise, both physiologically and behavioristically, are far from simple.

An interesting problem of a partially conflicting sensory pattern is 'the Meynert scheme' of the child and the candle-flame, which has become generally familiar owing to its having been quoted by James.* Meynert aims to show by a diagram how a child learns not to put his finger into a candle-flame. Two original reflexes are assumed: one in which the visual image of the candle causes the child's finger to go out to touch the flame; the other in which the painful heat on the finger causes the child's arm to be withdrawn. A fanciful series of nerve-paths, fabricated in the interests of the 'association theory,' purports to show why after once burning himself the child will in future put out his hand, on seeing a candle, but draw it back again *before* he burns himself. The explanation is beautifully accomplished by begging the whole

* The Principles of Psychology." New York, 1890, Vol. I, pp. 24-7.

question; that is, by resting the 'explanation' on certain time (and strength) relations between the two reflexes of extension and retraction—relations which neither diagram nor text accounts for. In fact, apart from the passage in which the whole question is begged, both diagram and text show that on every subsequent occasion the child will infallibly put out his hand, burn it, and then withdraw it, just as he had done the first time; for the reflex path for extending the hand is the shorter and the better established of the two, and it remains entirely vague as to how the impulse to withdraw shall arrive in time to save the hand.

But Meynert's explanation is not only unsuccessful, it is wrong in its intent. If achieved, it would show that a child once burned will on merely seeing a candle, and before it feels the candle's heat, draw back its hand. And this, Meynert thinks, is the process of learning. Whereas in fact a child that shrinks on merely *seeing* a candle has not *learned* anything; it has acquired a morbid fear. So far from being a step in learning, such a reaction will gravely impede the child in acquiring the use of this innocent utensil. It is true that one severe ex-

THE PHYSIOLOGY OF WISHES 71

perience of being burned can establish the morbid cringing at the mere sight of fire, but every teacher knows how disastrous this is to a child's progress; and the mechanism of such a response will not be found in any such figment of the imagination as that which Meynert adduces.* I know of nothing in this 'Meynert scheme' that tallies with fact, and, as James well says, it is " a mere scheme " and " anything but clear in detail." Nothing but the authority of the association theory ever loaned it plausibility.

The normal process of learning to deal with a candle is the process of establishing a response to an object which is both luminous and hot, if we consider only the two properties so far brought in question. The successful response will be one which is controlled directly by the actual properties of the candle, for this alone means precision and nicety in handling it. The normal child learns the properties of objects, without acquiring a fear of these properties; for fear is *not* ' wholesome.' The case in hand is simple. The child has in fact the

* Theodor Meynert was an Austrian. And in both Austria and Germany, despite the efforts of Froebel, the tradition survives that fear is a normal and necessary ingredient of the learning process.

two original tendencies, to put out its hand to touch any pretty, bright object, and to draw back its hand when the nerves of pain are stimulated. But these are at first not coördinated; and co-ordination (learning) is the establishment of a just balance between the openness of the two paths; where 'just' means proportioned to the actual properties of the candle. On first seeing a candle the child puts out its hand; the second reaction (of withdrawal) is touched off by stimulation of the heat-pain nerves in the hand,* and the moment at which this shall happen depends on the sensitiveness of the heat-pain end-organs, and the openness of the path connecting them with the muscles that retract the arm; of which probably the openness of path is the modifiable factor. The warmth of the candle begins to stimulate this retraction reflex, and stimulates it more, and at an increasing rate of increase, as the hand approaches the candle. All that is needed to save the child from burning its hand, and this is what Meynert's scheme aims to explain, is an openness of the retraction reflex path sufficient to stop the hand before it actually reaches

* Whether the organs of heat and pain are identical or distinct, the stimulation and sensation, is a single continuous series running from warmth to heat and pain.

THE PHYSIOLOGY OF WISHES 73

the flame. If the act of extension excited through the eye is not too impetuous, the retraction reflex will from the outset protect the hand; but if the former is a very open path, the advancing arm may get a momentum which the retraction reflex will not be sufficiently quick and strong to counterbalance in time to save the hand from being burned. A few repetitions of the experience will give this retraction path an openness which will safeguard the hand for the future; and this process is aided by the prolonged pain yielded by a burn, which continues the retraction stimulus for a considerable period and so 'wears' down the retraction path more than a great many merely momentary stimuli could do. In this way a single experience of burning is often sufficient for all time. Thus experience establishes a balance between the two opposed reflexes, of extension and of pain avoidance, such that the organism carries on its further examination of the candle in safety. If it be thought that this balance will never come about because each repetition will 'wear' the path for extension as much as that for retraction, it must be remembered, firstly, that the prolonged pain stimulation applies only to the latter path; and, secondly, that the opening, or '*Bahnung*,' of reflex paths is, like almost all processes in nature, a process which proceeds most rapidly at first. It is 'asymptotic.' The passage of a first nervous impulse over a path of high resistance 'wears' it down more than the same impulse would wear an already opened tract: just as the first five pedestrians across a snow-covered field do more toward making a path than do the next twenty-five.

The explanation which I have given does not account for all varieties of the learning process, of course, nor for the child's 'concept' of a candle. But it explains, I believe, how in point of fact a child learns not to burn its hands, and this is all that the fantastic Meynert scheme undertakes to do. The mechanism of learning is by no means understood as yet; that is to say, that the manner in which reflex paths are integrated to produce the more complicated forms of behavior is still a matter for investigation. Yet from the observation of behavior itself certain important facts have already been made out. One of these is that the principle of the mutual interference of opposed reflexes and the mutual augmentation of synenergic reflexes holds throughout. This principle, indeed, although it becomes endlessly complicated and in some cases (as in the production of reflex stepping and other alternating movements by means of 'reciprocal innervation') is even partly obscured, seems to be the one general formula for reflex integration. This can be seen in operation in all cases of behavior from the most purely reflex to the most highly 'conscious.' Thus, just as the leaves of certain plants, which are subject to the two impulses of facing the sunlight but also of avoiding desiccating heat, will spread themselves out broadly toward the sun in the morning and afternoon, but in the heat of noonday will partially fold up, so under the teacher's eye the pugnacious impulse of the small boy is subdued to the furtive expedient of the spit-ball; and so, too, the man who yearns for worldly power but yet in *personal* contact with his fellows is unconquerably timid will become a renowned inventor, or a shrewd manipulator of stock-markets, or in politics will work into some important position ' *behind* the throne.'

Another feature incidental to the integration of reflexes, which is seen from the observation of behavior, is what I may call the *recession of the stimulus.* This is a point not insisted on by Freud, but one which is of vast importance to a clear understanding of the dynamic psychology which Freud has so immensely furthered. The single reflex is of course always touched off by some stimulus, and if only reflex process is in question the immediate stimulus is the inciting and controlling factor. But where even two reflexes are working together to produce specific response or behavior, the case is altered: the stimulus is now merely an agent, a part of a higher process. We have already seen this in the case of our water animal which was enabled by two eye-spots and two fins to swim toward light. Now this light toward which it swims is not the *immediate* stimulus, which rather is the light quanta which at any moment have entered the cells of the eye-spot. And one could not describe what the animal *as a whole* is *doing* in terms of the immediate stimuli; but this can be described only in terms of the environing *objects* toward which the animal's response is directed. This is precisely the distinction between reflex action and specific response or behavior. As the number of component reflexes involved in response increases, the immediate stimulus itself

THE PHYSIOLOGY OF WISHES 77

recedes further and further from view as the significant factor.

This is very evident in the case of the bee. We may grant with Bethe that the bee is only, in the last analysis, a reflex mechanism. But it is a very complex one, and when we are studying the bee's behavior we are studying an organism which by means of integrated reflexes has become enabled to respond specifically to the objects of its environment. It may be doubted whether Bethe, or any other of the biologists, fully realizes the significance of this; fully realizes, that is, how completely in behavior the stimulus recedes from its former position of importance. To study the behavior of the bee is of course to put the question, "What is the bee doing?" This is a plain scientific question. Yet if we should put it thus to Bethe, his answer would probably be: "It is doing of course a great many things; now its visual organ is stimulated and it darts toward a flower; now its olfactory organ is stimulated and it goes for a moment to rub antennæ with another bee of its own hive; and so forth." But this is not an answer. We ask, "What is the bee doing?" And we are told, "Now its visual . . . and now its olfactory, . . ." etc., etc. With a little persistence we could probably get Bethe to say, "Why, the *bee* isn't doing anything." Whereas an unbiased observer can see plainly enough that "The *bee* is laying by honey in its home."

My point is that the often too materialistically-minded biologist is so fearful of meeting a certain bogy, the 'psychic,' that he hastens to analyze every case of behavior into its component reflexes without venturing first to observe it as a whole. In this way he fails to note the recession of the stimulus and the infallibly objective reference of behavior. He does not see that in any case of behavior no immediate sense stimulus whatsoever will figure in a straightforward and exact description of what the creature is doing: and 'What?' is the first question which science puts to any phenomenon. This was the case even in the first instance which we looked at (p. 52), where two eye-spots and two vibratory cilia enabled an animal to *swim toward a light*. It is equally true in the cases of the rootlet, and of the planarian which responds specifically to an amount of change, or even a rate of change. It is a thousand times more marked in the case of the bee, for here not only would it not

THE PHYSIOLOGY OF WISHES 79

be possible to describe what the bee does in terms of sensory stimuli, but also in much of the bee's conduct it would not be possible to point out any *physical* object on which the bee's activities turn or toward which they are directed. It lays up a store of honey in its home. If we suppose that here the parental hive is the physical object around which the bee's activities center, we soon find ourselves wrong, for when the swarm migrates the bee knows the old hive no more but continues its busy life of hoarding in some other locality. The fact is that the specific object on which the bee's activities are focused, and of which they are a function, its 'home,' is a very complex *situation*, neither hive, locality, coworkers, nor yet flowers and honey, but a situation of which all of these are the related components. In short we cannot do justice to the case of the bee, unless we admit that he is the citizen of a state, and that this phrase, instead of being a somewhat fanciful metaphor or analogy, is the literal description of what the bee demonstrably is and does. Many biologists shy at such a description; they believe that these considerations should be left to Vergil and to M. Maeterlinck, while they themselves deem it safer to deal with the bee's olfactory and visual organs. They will not describe the bee's behavior as a whole, will not observe what mere reflexes when coöperating integrally in one organism can accomplish, because they fear, at bottom, to encounter that bogy which philosophers have set in their way, the 'subjective' or the 'psychic.' They need not be afraid of this, for all that they have to do is to describe in the most objective manner possible what the bee is doing.

But our present point is that even two reflexes acting within one organism bring it about that the organism's behavior is no longer describable in terms of the immediate sensory stimulus, but as a function of objects and of situations in the environment, and even of such aspects of objects as positions, directions, degrees of concentration, rates of change, etc. While as the number of integrated reflexes increases, in the higher organisms, the immediate stimulus recedes further and further from view, and is utterly missing in an exact description (merely that) of what the organism does.

Thus it comes about that in the description of the behavior of creatures as complicated as human beings it has been quite forgotten that sensory stimuli and reflexes are still at the bottom of it *all*. Indeed, such a suggestion has only to be made and it will be instantly repudiated, especially by those philosophers and psychologists who deem themselves the accredited guardians of historic truth. In other words, the study of the integration of reflexes has been so neglected, and it is indeed difficult, that we have come to believe that an unfathomable gulf exists between the single reflex movement and the activities of conscious, thinking creatures. The gap in our knowledge is held to be a gap in the continuity of nature. And yet if we face the matter frankly, we see that history, biography, fiction, and the drama are all descriptions of what men do, of human behavior. We are wont to say, " Ah, yes, but the true interest of these things lies in what the men are meanwhile *thinking*." So be it. But are thought and behavior so *toto caelo* different? And what did Spinoza mean by saying that " The will and the intellect are one and the same "? And, further, have those who so confidently assert that thought is a principle distinct from integrated reflex activity ever succeeded in telling what 'thought' is? We meet here, of course, the profoundest question in psychology, and the one which for more than a hundred years has been the central problem of philosophy—What is cognition? Or, Is cognition different in principle from integrated reflex behavior?

I must state that Freud has never raised this question in so explicit a form. He has also not answered it. But by discovering for us the way in which the 'thoughts' of men react on one another, in actual concrete fact, he has given us the key that fits one of the most ancient and most baffling of locks. What I shall say in the remainder of this section is confessedly more than Freud has said; it is, however, as I believe, the inevitable and almost immediate deduction from what he has said. This view of mind as integrated reflex behavior is subversive of much that is traditional in philosophy and psychology, and particularly of the dualistic dogma which holds that the mechanical and spiritual principles, so unmistakable in our universe, are utterly alien to each other, and even largely incompatible. This newer view, however, instead of being subversive, is unexpectedly and categorically confirmatory of certain ancient doctrines of morals and of freedom:—verities which have been well-nigh forgotten in a so-called 'scientific' age.

THE PHYSIOLOGY OF WISHES

Let us consider, then, the higher forms of behavior, in human beings, and the question of consciousness and thought.*

If one sees a man enter a railway station, purchase a ticket, and then pass out and climb on to a train, one feels that it is clear enough what the man is doing, but it would be far more interesting to know what he is thinking. One sees clearly that he is taking a train, but one cannot see his thoughts or his intentions and these contain the 'secret' of his actions. And thus we come to say that the conscious or subjective is a peculiar realm, private to the individual, and open only to his *in*trospection. It is apart from the world of objective fact. Suppose, now, one were to apply the same line of reasoning to an event of inanimate nature. At dawn the sun rises above the eastern ridge of hills. This is the plain fact, and it is not of itself too interesting. But what is the 'secret' behind such an occurrence? "Why this is, as everybody knows, that the sun is the god Helios who every

* This new theory of cognition can of course be treated here only in outline. I have written further of it under the title of "Response and Cognition" in *The Journal of Philosophy, Psychology, and Scientific Methods*, 1915, Vol. XII, pp. 365-372; 393-409. The article is reprinted as a Supplement to this book.

morning drives his chariot up out of the East, and he has some magnificent purpose in mind. We cannot tell just what it is because his thoughts and purposes are subjective and not open to our observation. We suspect, however, that he is paying court to Ceres, and so cheers on by his presence the growing crops." Or again, the same line of reasoning as used in a somewhat later age. The stream flows through the field, leaps the waterfall, and goes foaming onward down the valley. The fact is that it has always done so. And the secret? " Well, they used to say that the stream was a daughter of Neptune and that she was hurrying past to join her father. We know better than that now; we know that water always seeks its own level, and the only secret about it is that the water is urged on from behind by an impulse which some call the *vis viva*. We've never seen this *vis viva*, for it is invisible; but it is the secret of all inanimate motion; and of course it must be there, for otherwise nothing would move."

It has taken man ages to learn that the gaps in his knowledge of observed fact cannot be filled by creatures of the imagination. It is the most precious achievement of the physical sciences that

THE PHYSIOLOGY OF WISHES 85

the 'secrets behind' phenomena lie in the phenomena and are to be found out by *observing* the *phenomena* and in no other way. The 'mental' sciences have yet to learn this lesson. Continued observation of the rising and setting sun revealed that the secret behind was not the gallantry of Helios, but the rotation of our earth which, by simple geometry, caused the sun relatively to ourselves to rise in the East. Continued observation of water showed that neither a nature god nor yet a *vis viva* is the secret behind the flowing stream; but that the stream is flowing as directly as the surface of the earth permits, toward *the center of the earth*. And that this is merely a special instance of the fact that all masses move toward one another. There is indeed a mystery behind such motion, but science calls this mystery neither Helios, Neptune, nor *vis viva*, but simply motion; and science will penetrate this mystery by more extended observation of motion. Now the inscrutable 'thought behind' the actions of a man, which is the invisible secret of those actions, is another myth, like the myths of the nature gods and the *vis viva*. Not that there are not actual thoughts, but tradition has turned thought into a myth by utterly misconceiving it and locating in the wrong place.

On seeing the man purchase a ticket at the railway station, we felt that there was more behind this action, 'thoughts' that were the invisible secret of his movements. Suppose, instead, we inquire whether the more is not ahead. More is to come; let us watch the man further. He enters the train, which carries him to a city. There he proceeds to an office, on the door of which we read 'Real Estate.' Several other men are in this office; a document is produced; our man takes a sum of money from his pocket and gives this to one of the other men, and this man with some of the others signs the document. This they give to our man, and with it a bunch of keys. All shake hands, and the man whom we are watching departs. He goes to the railway station and takes another train, which carries him to the town where we first saw him. He walks through several streets, stops before an empty house, takes out his bunch of keys, and makes his way into the house. Not long afterwards several vans drive up in front, and the men outside proceed to take household furniture off the vans and into the house. Our man inside indicates

THE PHYSIOLOGY OF WISHES 87

where each piece is to be placed. He later gives the men from the vans money.

All this we get by observing what the man does, and without in any way appealing to the 'secret' thoughts of the man. If we wish to know more of what he is doing we have only to observe him more. Suppose, however, that we had appealed to his inner thoughts to discover the 'secret' of his movements, when we first saw him buying a ticket at the railway station. We approach him and say, "Sir, I am a philosopher and extremely anxious to know what you are doing, and of course I cannot learn that unless you will tell me what you are thinking." "Thinking?" he may reply, if he condones our guileless impertinence. "Why, I am thinking that it's a plaguey hot day, and I wish I had made my morning bath five degrees colder, and drunk less of that hot-wash that my wife calls instant coffee." "Was that all?" "Yes, that was all until I counted my change; and then I heard the train whistle.—Here it is. Good-by! And good luck to your philosophy!"

Thought is often a mere irrelevance, a surface embroidery on action. What is more important, the very best that the man could have told us would have been *no better* than what we have learned by watching the man. At best he could have told us, " I am intending to buy a house and to get my furniture in to-day "; exactly what we have observed. And if he told us his further intentions, these in turn could be as completely learned by watching his movements; and *more* reliably, since men do both think and speak lies.

Freud makes, however, the further point that thought, that is, conscious thought, is so little complete as to be scarcely any index to a man's character or deeds. This is Freud's doctrine of the unconscious; although Freud is by no means the first to discover or to emphasize the unconscious. A man's conscious thoughts, feelings, and desires are determined by unconscious thoughts or ' wishes ' which lie far deeper down, and which the upper, conscious man knows nothing of. I have illustrated this doctrine at length in the first part of this volume. In fact, conscious thought is merely the surface foam of a sea where the real currents are well beneath the surface. It is an error, then, to suppose that the ' secret behind ' a man's actions lies in those thoughts which he (and he alone) can ' introspectively survey.' We shall presently see

THE PHYSIOLOGY OF WISHES

that it is an error to contrast thought with action at all.

But what are we to do when 'thought' has receded to so impregnable a hiding-place? We are to admit, I think, that we have misunderstood the nature of thought, and predicated so much that is untrue of it, that what we have come to call 'thought' is a pure myth. We are to say with William James:* "I believe that 'consciousness,' when once it has evaporated to this estate of pure diaphaneity, is on the point of disappearing altogether. It is the name of a nonentity, and has no right to a place among first principles. Those who still cling to it are clinging to a mere echo, the faint rumor left behind by the disappearing 'soul' upon the air of philosophy." This is the keynote of his Radical Empiricism, the principle that of all those which he enunciated was dearest to him; and it is his final repudiation of dualism. With this we return to the facts.

It is just one error which has prevented us from seeing that the study of what men *do*, i.e., how they 'behave,' comprises the entire field of psy-

* "Essays in Radical Empiricism." New York, 1912, p. 2.

chology. And that is the failure to distinguish essence from accident. If one holds out one's hand and lets fall a rubber ball, it moves down past the various parts of one's person and strikes the floor; now it is opposite one's breast, now at the level of the table-top, now at the level of the chair-seat, and now it rests on the floor. This, we say, is what the ball does, and all this is as true as it is irrelevant. For if the same ball had been dropped by some other means from the same point it would have fallen in just the same way if neither oneself, nor the table, nor the chair had been there. It was all accident that it fell past one's breast and past the table; accident even that it hit the floor, for had there been no floor there it would have continued to fall. What the ball is *essentially* doing, although it took science a long time to find this out, is *moving toward the center of the earth;* and in this lies significance, for if the earth's mass were displaced or abolished, the motion of the ball would indeed be concomitantly displaced or abolished. Mathematics and science conveniently designate that which is thus essential in any process as 'function.' It is accident that the ball moves parallel to the table-leg, for essentially the movement of the ball is a function of the earth's center. *This* is what the ball is *really ' doing.'* We have adumbrated this same fact in connection with the bee. It is in the present respect accidental that the bee sips at this flower, or that; pluck them aside and the bee will turn as well to other flowers. What is, however, not accidental is that the bee is laying up honey in its home; for the bee's life-activities are a function of its home,—and home is a complicated but purely objective state of things. All this is but a different aspect of that which I have called the recession of the stimulus; the latter giving place, as reflexes become more and more integrated, to objects and to *relations* between objects as that of which the total body-activity is a function.

Now it is the same case with the man whom we saw buying a railway ticket. What he is thinking at the moment is likely to be a most irrelevant gloss on what he is actually doing, and will be far from being the ' secret ' of his movements. At the very most favorable moment his thought can do no more than reveal to us what he is doing; for notoriously introspection gives us no clew as to *how* we achieve even the least voluntary movement. Therefore what the man is doing is the sole question to be considered. But on the other hand, while it is true that the man is buying a ticket it is only a subordinate and insignificant matter, for essentially the man is purchasing a house, and this latter statement shows us that of which the man's total behavior is a true function. The purchase of a railway ticket is as accidental to this process as a body's striking the floor is irrelevant to the law of gravitation; and if there were no railway in existence the man would purchase his house, and go to secure his deed by stage-coach, chaise, or on his legs. Just as the stimulus recedes, so the component activities recede from their primary position in the total process, as integration advances. Both stimulus and component process are there and are necessary, but they are only parts of a larger whole.

These considerations make it clear, I trust, why the dualistic philosophical view, which contrasts physical motion with a secret, inscrutable, 'psychical' process 'behind,' is mischievous.* It totally ignores the work of integration, and to assuage

* The view which I am outlining has, per contra, nothing to do with 'materialism,' as I have shown at length in "The Concept of Consciousness."

THE PHYSIOLOGY OF WISHES 93

this ignorance it fabricates a myth. With that view falls also the entire subject of 'psycho-physical parallelism'; which was a complete misapprehension from the outset. It is not that we have two contrasted worlds, the 'objective' and the 'subjective'; there is but one world, the objective, and that which we have hitherto not understood, have dubbed therefore the 'subjective,' are the subtler workings of integrated objective mechanisms.

The same considerations give light on another, though cognate, issue. The man who buys a ticket is said to do so in the interest of some 'end' which he has in mind. In this way action is, again, contrasted (as the 'means') with the mental secret of action (the 'end'). This is an unfortunate way of looking at the matter, since in reality, as I have tried to show, that which is so contrasted with the subordinate action ('means'), and is said to be a mentally entertained 'end' and quite different in nature from the means, is after all precisely another action—the purchase of a home. It is not true that we do something in order to attain a dead and static 'end'; we do something as the neecssary but subordinate moment in the *doing* of something more comprehensive. The true comparison then is not between deed or means and thought or end, but between part deed and whole deed. This is of importance, and we shall consider it again; but I will point out, in passing, that without this fallacy of 'ends' we should never have been afflicted with that fantastic whimsy called 'hedonistic ethics'; which, I incline to think, is responsible for much of modern deviltry.

We return now to the main line of our argument. It is clear that this *function* which behavior or conduct is of the external situation is the very same thing which Freud deals with under the name of 'wish.' It is a course of action which the body takes or is prepared (by motor set) to take with reference to objects, relations, or events in the environment. The prophetic quality of thought which makes it seem that thought is the hidden and inner secret of conduct is due to the fact that thought is the preceding labile interplay of motor settings which goes on almost constantly, and which differs from overt conduct in that the energy involved is too small to produce gross bodily movements. This is a piece of nature's economy.

Now in this wish or function we have the pure

THE PHYSIOLOGY OF WISHES 95

essence of human will, and of the soul itself. No distinction can be found between function, wish, and purpose; in every case we are dealing with a dynamic relation between the individual's living body, as subject of the relation (or mathematically speaking the 'dependent variable'), and some environmental fact, as object of the relation (or 'independent variable'). The mechanism of the body incorporates the wish or purpose. And this view gives a concrete meaning to Aristotle's dictum that the soul is the '*form*' or "entelechy of a natural body endowed with the capacity of life."* The living body through a long process of organization has come at length to 'embody' purpose. But the soul is of course always and forever the *purpose* that is embodied, and not the mere matter (Aristotle's 'potentiality') that as a mechanism embodies. The distinction is the same as that between the design which an inventor patents and the steel and brass in which the plan is tangibly realized.

Such a view of the soul departs widely from the academic dogmas of the present day and from popular psychology; and it has the apparent

* "De Anima," 412a.

novelty that any restatement of the views of Plato and Aristotle must have in an age which has forgotten the classics. One or two further deviations from current psychological notions must be briefly mentioned. The first and most important is in regard to 'consciousness.' This actually figures in all modern discussions as a substance which, contrasted with the substance of matter, is that of which sensations, ideas, and thoughts are composed: the ego, mind, and soul are thought to be made of it, it is the 'subjective' essence, and the question of cognition is concerned with the relations between consciousness and matter. In the view now before us, consciousness and 'the subjective as such' are done away with. Consciousness is not a substance but a relation—the relation between the living organism and the environment to which it specifically responds; of which its behavior is found to be this or that constant function; or, in other words, to which its purposes refer. This is the relation of awareness, and the cognitive relation. There will be no consciousness except in a situation where *both* living organism and environment are present and where the functional relation already described exists between them. It has always been admitted that cognition involves a knower and a known, and if we look for these in this situation, we see at once that the body is the knower, and the environing objects responded to are the known. In short, those objects or aspects toward which we respond, of which our purposes are functions—these are the 'contents of consciousness.' And these immediately, not some pale '*re*presentations' thereof. This is a return to the obvious fact that what a man knows are the actual things around him, the objects and events with which he has to deal; it is a return also to Aristotle, who said, "Actual knowledge is identical with its object"; * and again, "The mind *is* the thing when actually thinking it." † Here it is of secondary importance whether there is overt and grossly visible conduct or only the less energetic play of motor setting and attitude, for the two are equally describable only as functions of something in the outside situation; and that about which a man thinks is clearly, even for introspection, numerically identical with that upon which his actions turn, and with that which, when he comes near enough, he sees and handles.

* "De Anima," 431*a*. † *Ibidem*, 431*b*.

Thought is, however, more than the object thought about: there is active thinking about the objects. If we look once more at the least manifold in which cognition occurs—a living organism in, and responsive to, an environment—we see that this further active element is the active play of motor attitude, which eventually resolves itself into the less labile but more forceful phenomenon, conduct. Thus *thought is latent course of action with regard to environment* (i.e., is motor setting), or a procession of such attitudes. But we have already found that will is also course of action with regard to environment, so that the only difference between thought and volition is one of the intensity of nerve impulse that plays through the sensori-motor arcs—a difference of minimal importance for either psychology *or ethics*. From this appears the literal truth of Spinoza's dictum that "The will and the intellect are one and the same"; a saying that is verifiable on many sides, and one which early moralists recognize in such maxims as, "As a man thinketh in his heart, so is he"; but one which, on the other hand, is made unintelligible in the scheme of the mind offered by current psychology.

The scheme that I have been suggesting could be

THE PHYSIOLOGY OF WISHES

elucidated and fortified by the consideration of attention, memory, emotion, illusions, and the other phenomena studied by psychology. But I have discussed these at some length elsewhere,* and enough has been said, I think, to show what sort of a dynamic theory of will and cognition Freud's doctrine of the ' wish,' as I believe, implies. We have seen that the wish is purpose embodied in the mechanism of a living organism, that it is necessarily a wish about, or a purpose regarding, some feature of the environment; so that a total situation comprising *both organism and environment* is always involved. We have seen that will, thought, and the object of knowledge are all integral and inseparable parts of this total situation. Inseparable because, if organism and environment are sundered, the cognitive relation is dissolved, and merely matter remains; precisely as only water remains when a rainbow is pulled apart. Mind is a relation and not a substance.

* " Response and Cognition." *The Journal of Philosophy, Psychology, and Scientific Methods.* 1915, Vol. XII, pp. 365-372; 393-409. Cf. Supplement.

"The Concept of Consciousness." George Allen and Macmillan, 1914.

"The Place of Illusory Experience in a Realistic World." An essay in " The New Realism." Macmillan, 1912.

CHAPTER III

THE WISH IN ETHICS

If the wish or purpose is, so to say, the unit of conduct, it is clear that ethics ought to take the wish as its fundamental unit of discourse, whatsoever its further argument is to be as to the nature of the good or the source of moral sanction. But 'wish' is here as unfortunate a word as Freud could have chosen, since it seems to signify desire for or interest in some 'end.' I have tried to show that an analysis of Freud's wish implies nothing of the sort; that the wish is a purpose or course of action with regard to the environment and that it contemplates no end whatsoever, just as time itself infers no end. The only semblance of 'end' is found where one purpose is yoked into the service of another purpose, and here the latter might roughly be called the 'end' of the former; yet only roughly and inexactly so, since the whole is process and the subordinate purposes are only its articulate phases. Avoiding this misapprehen-

THE WISH IN ETHICS 101

sion we have to see whether conduct, which is compounded of such purposes, has ethical significance.

An innate tendency or purpose of an infant is to put out its hand to touch fire. If the mother is by, she holds back the hand (*her* purpose) before it reaches the flame. There is a hint for the child, here, of right and wrong. If the mother guards the child unremittingly, and every time restrains the hand before the uncomfortable warmth begins to stimulate the child's own tendency to withdraw, the child will never be burned and may eventually (in a way to be described) acquire the habit of stopping short before reaching the flame. But this cautious conduct will not be guided by (be a function of) the heat of the flame, for the child has had no experience of this. The child's general conduct toward fire will then be partly a function of the immediate properties of fire (its color, position, shape, etc.); but partly also of a something else (really its mother), which may or may not figure explicitly in the child's field of consciousness. The mother has set a barrier between the child and a portion of reality; and forever after the child will be in some measure impeded in its dealings with fire. An inhibition of which the source or sanction is thus not intrinsic is precisely, I suppose, a tabu.

Or again, if an equally unremitting mother lets the child put out its hand toward the flame and takes care only that the hand by too great momentum or an accidental lurch does not actually come into the flame, the child will not be burned and its own mechanism of withdrawal will be exercised not through the mother's interference but through the direct action of the flame's heat. The child's conduct toward fire becomes integrated, and is solely a function of the actual properties of fire. Ten years later you shall hear the first mother shouting, " Bobbie, don't you dare put your hand so near the lamp, and if you touch those matches again your father will whip you." And the second mother will be saying, " Bobbie, go get the matches now and light the lamp, and set it down on the center-table."

Here the reader may feel that I egregiously beg the question by a couple of cheap improvisations. Let us see: for here we come to the most essential point in Freud. The first mother has pushed back the child's hand *before* the child's own mechanism of withdrawal was stimulated (by the heat). The

THE WISH IN ETHICS 103

child is frustrated, but not instructed; and it is in the situation where, later on in life, we say to ourselves, "If at first you don't succeed, try, try again!" The child tries and tries again, and mother is kept busy. This effectively exercises the child's tendency to move toward the flame, and leaves *undeveloped* its equally inborn tendency to withdraw from heat. In short, the mother is actually ingraining the very tendency which she wishes to curb. Why, then, does her method seem to her to produce caution in the child? Because if she perseveres for a year or so (as she will), the child matures and can respond to a more complicated situation, which is flame-and-mother in constellation. This conjunction it directly experiences, and it learns that when mother is around it can't touch fire. Unfortunately, however, this is for him an intrinsic property of mother, and not of fire. There is the evil. Yet this is a genuine quality of the mother, and the child learns *this* without tabu, so that when mother and flame are together it perceives the situation where flame cannot be touched. And now, if the mother has not succumbed to worry meanwhile, she is gratified at having 'taught' the child caution. In reality she has done only this:—she has deepened by habit the tendency to reach out toward flame, has left unexercised the conservative tendency to withdraw from heat, has waited for the child to grow up sufficiently to learn that the non-touchability of flame is a property of herself, has worried herself into a nagging mother, and has prematurely got the child to respond to *herself* as an *object* of the environment, with qualities of her own and needing suitably to be studied and dealt with. What is worst of all, if she is spared to continue her misguided watchfulness until the youth's plastic period is passed, he will have such an insatiable tendency to play with fire, in her absence, that no amount of *actual burns* will ever correct it.

All this is a paradigm of Freudian morals. In order to introduce some convenient terms, I will put the matter more technically. The mother's hand that stays the child's hand *before* the child's innate tendency to withdraw from heat has been stimulated is a barrier between the child and the flame. To this barrier, the mother's hand, the child has already acquired various modes of response; it now acquires another, to draw back from the mother's hand-in-front-of-flame, just as it

THE WISH IN ETHICS 105

learns to halt before a high fence. The mother's hand '*suppresses*' the child's innate tendency to touch the fire. But the child's withdrawal becomes a withdrawal from the mother's hand and not, as it ought to be, a response to (or function of) the flame itself. Freud, like others before him, calls this '*dissociation*': The precautionary response which should be 'associated' with fire is dissociated therefrom, and transferred to something else; in our case to the mother. Take this mother away, and the child knows no caution with regard to fire. All responses to the mother become integrated into a group or '*complex*,' and those toward flame into another complex. The two complexes are not entirely out of relation to each other, yet each has more internal cohesiveness than it has cohesion with the other complex. Between the two there is relative dissociation. We are to bear in mind that the same innate tendency to " touch the pretty flame " remains, and has been strengthened by the child's trying over and over to touch it, simply because the mother prevented the child from learning on its very *first* trial that flame is painfully hot. And let us note also that if there is any question here of right and wrong conduct on the part of the child it rests *solely* on the fact that fire burns; and further, that the misguided mother has undertaken to arrogate to herself this bit of what should be her child's experience, to transfer the rôle of truth to her own person. She has not trusted the truth.

The other mother was equally tender, and far wiser. She saw to it that no accidental lurch or fall brought her child's hand into the flame. But she let the child follow its own bent of reaching toward the flame until its own other tendency to avoid heat was stimulated and exercised by the direct fact of heat in the flame. Her child will not be actually burned any more than the other. By thus trusting the truth it takes about two days to establish in a normal child cautious conduct with regard to fire. A normal child of the same age can in about two years' time be taught that you are always an obstacle between it and fire, and that fire is *not hot*. For the injudicious mother has in deed told this lie to the child. The wise mother, furthermore, has not put herself in the position of an alien force frustrating the child; and certainly it is desirable that for several years at least a child should not have its attention directly drawn to either mother or father as an object more distinct from itself

THE WISH IN ETHICS 107

than its own arms or legs. Non-frustration is the condition for *sympathy:* frustration, obviously, for antipathy. The parent must decide whether he *ever* wishes to dissolve the sympathy between himself and a child.

We have now to look a little more closely at the workings of suppression. At the age of ten our boy has too freely partaken of doughnuts and is going through the motions appropriate to stomachache. He has not done 'wrong,' but is merely getting experience of a new object. The doughnuts are like the fire of his earlier days, except that their noxiousness is deferred, and not, like a burn, immediate; and that it depends on the quantity partaken of. It will take longer than before to establish suitable behavior in the presence of doughnuts. In time, however, this would establish itself without outside interference. A new element in this situation is what we may call *appetite.* Since the organism requires for its continuance certain things from the environment, nature has established a mechanism such that the *absence* of these requisites acts as an *internal stimulus,* and the whole organism is caused to move restlessly about until the missing ingredient chances to impinge on a sense-organ of the animal, and is forthwith appropriated. Thus if there is too little oxygen in the surrounding medium, it necessarily comes about that there is too high a percentage of carbon dioxide in the animal's blood and this acts as a specific internal stimulus firstly to speed up the activities of heart and lungs, and secondly to irritate the nervous system generally, thus setting the animal into restless motion. As development proceeds and specific responses are established to various elements of the environment, these responses become integrated with the internal deficit stimuli, and the general nervous irritation is drawn into specific motor channels: the general motor restlessness becomes a specific course of action. And when this point is reached we say that the animal " knows what it wants." There are two elemental appetites, the nutritive (including that for oxygen) and the sexual; possibly more. Now in connection with appetites it is perfectly just to speak of ' desire ' and ' *end* '; but this must not lead us to forget that the special conduct determined by appetite remains, equally with all other conduct, a *function* of *environment;* still less should this case mislead us, as I believe the majority of writers on ethics have been misled, into believing that desire and end reveal the general pattern of human will. This would be, I must insist, to mistake an important yet only special case for the general law. The above makes clear, I trust, how 'desire' is defined without recourse to subjective categories, and how 'desire' for 'ends' arises through mechanical integration.

And our ten-year-old has an appetite for doughnuts. We will say that his first feast with its attendant penalty occurred through a parental oversight, and that the subsequent parental injunctions coincided so exactly with the course of moderation already impressed, and through painful hours continuously deepened, by the lad's digestive apparatus, that the doughnut question never arose again. But five years later he encounters tobacco. Here the disastrous consequences (in part stunted growth) are so serious, so deferred, and so irremediable that the boy can by no means be allowed to make the trial for himself. A question of morals is going to arise; and let us again be quite clear at the outset that, whatever complications may come up, the ultimate sanction for the 'right' course of action in this regard will be nothing but the *fact* that tobacco does injure growing lads. The father explains to the boy the injurious action of tobacco, and that therefore it will be 'not right' for him to use tobacco until he has attained his full growth; after which time the effect of tobacco will be somewhat different and the lad will then decide the matter for himself. Here I assume the effective use of written and spoken 'signs.' The mechanism of signs is as yet but little understood, and it is not a thing to be merely speculated on. What is certain is that in the course of integration outer objects come to be responded to by specific gestures and modulations of the voice—responses which have a purely social significance; that these responses become somehow integrated with the other, more practical, responses to the same objects, respectively; and that, as a result, such signs uttered by one person and perceived by another serve to touch off, or indeed to organize, the same responses in the second person as would have been touched off or organized in the latter if he had had the same experience with the objects signified as the first person has had. It is a marvelous function and one that is susceptible of grave derangements.

The situation before us needs analysis. In the first place, tobacco appeals to no authentic appetite

THE WISH IN ETHICS 111

of the boy, in the sense above described. But it is an object of the environment, and at the stage of development now in question it evokes complicated specific responses of a sort which we somewhat loosely call curiosity and imitation. I believe that it cannot be said with certainty whether such responses do or do not derive additional impetus from the basic appetites. In any case it will be not far wrong to consider the tendency of a boy to investigate the possibilities of tobacco and to imitate the use which others make of it, as being like the tendency which he possessed as a baby to put out his hand toward fire. After the talk with his father two tendencies in the boy are stimulated: on the one hand are the former tendencies of curiosity and imitation; and on the other, his father's words "tobacco will injure you" and "it is *not right* for you to use it." (I pass over the possibility that the father has said, "I will punish you if you touch tobacco"; for this would reduce the case to precisely the type already considered, in which a mother undertook by force to restrain her child from experiencing the properties of fire.) The boy now faces a *dilemma;* and clearly a moral problem.

It is possible to view this as an issue between

'abstract' right and wrong, that is, to view the moral sanction involved as in some manner categorical. This would be, I think, to commit the fallacy of over-abstraction; and one notes that the systems of ethics which posit an *abstract* sanction for right conduct, never discover *what* 'right' is. In this way, pathetically enough, the upshot of academic ethics is merely a very learned interrogation point. We shall revert to this matter of morals *von oben herab*. In any case such an abstract position would not be the Freudian; and the inferable Freudian ethics is distinctly one *von unten hinauf;* as follows.

If the boy has hitherto found in his father a truth-telling man, the father's talk will have conveyed to the boy, not a 'father *says*,' but a 'tobacco *is*' (injurious). This item will then take its place as an integral part of the complex named tobacco. Language will have served its proper task, and there will be no dissociation, or transfer of 'injuriousness' from 'tobacco' to 'father.' The boy may still dabble with tobacco, but the first step at least is accomplished. And this step is indispensable, for if the lad is to benefit by the experience of others rather than experience the bitter

THE WISH IN ETHICS 113

truth for himself, there must be some source of information which shall be to the boy *fact* and not mere asseveration. This source should be preeminently the father and mother. Now Freud has shown, in an essay * which all parents might well read, that children are very early and very keenly cognizant of untruthfulness in their elders. This is not astonishing, although very generally ignored; for beyond question even dogs and cats distinguish between truthfulness and untruthfulness of deed (and sometimes even of word). Freud also shows that *one* untruthful word of father or mother will often undermine the child's confidence forever, and he urges on parents the necessity of quite unqualified truthfulness. I have talked with many parents of young children and have found but few who trust the truth sufficiently to deem it practicable with children. But parents need not waste breath to dub the truth ' sacred,' when they themselves do not trust it; and such parents have only themselves to thank when, in order to secure obedience, they have to resort to cajoleries, threats, whipping-posts,

---

* "Zur sexuellen Aufklärung der Kinder," in " Sammlung kleiner Schriften zur Neurosenlehre," 2te Folge. Deuticke, Leipzig, 1909, S. 151.

and such superstitions as '*abstract Right*." A little concrete rightness in the parent will go much further.* If, now, Bobbie's father is a truthful man, the next step will follow; if not, Bobbie will get elsewhere such information as he can, and the next step will still follow. This I prefer to describe, however, on the assumption that the father is known by his son to be a truth-teller. And let us not forget that a truth-telling father, like a hypocritical father, is as much an *object* of the child's environment as a thermometer, a clock, a seismo-

* Such pious perjury as the following, for instance, will never do. In regard to the instruction of children in matters of sex, one may read in a recent book—" a full insight into the psychology of sex is highly dangerous. Surely the boy should know only part of the facts! Surely it is permissible to lead him to believe that all women are more or less as we would have them be in an ideal world, and to allow men to appear to him as rather better in these respects than they actually are! The tree of knowledge cannot be robbed of its dangers," etc. (William McDougall: "An Introduction to Social Psychology," 8th edition. Methuen, London, 1914, pp. 420-421.) And then we wonder why our little lambs do not graze guilelessly beneath this parental Tree of Deliberate Misinformation; why Bobbie consults street gamins on many matters rather than his father; and why Bobbie soon says to himself, " Surely it is permissible to lead father to believe that I am rather better than I actually am, in fact that I am just as he would have me be in an ideal world!" Freud, at least, earnestly deplores such treachery in parents. A diet of untruth does not equip a child for the realities of life.

THE WISH IN ETHICS 115

graph, or an encyclopedia. And specific modes of response toward him are established by the same integrative mechanism.

The next step is more interesting than the first. The boy now faces a dilemma, to smoke or not to smoke; a dilemma that is comparable with the baby's, to touch or not to touch fire *after* having once felt its heat, for the function of language is such that the father's truthful words are in a measure the equivalent of an unpleasant experience with tobacco. But in this case the hindrance has not quite the positive and immediate urgency of heat-pain, and the second step enjoys a corresponding latitude. Now tobacco, in itself purely, appeals to no innate appetite, and I think it can be confidently asserted that the truthful father's warning will be sufficient to check the boy's passing whim of imitation, *unless* this latter is reënforced by *other* tendencies of a more intrinsic potency.

And it very possibly is so reënforced. For tobacco, like long trousers, figures in the paraphernalia of adults, and 'to act grown-up' is a very common boyish wish, or mode of behavior. This wish is one component of a large complex of interrelated responsive settings, the '*ego complex*,' or, as Shand, McDougall, and Prince prefer to say, the 'self-regarding sentiment.' It is apt to have such variant forms and associates as the wish to be independent, 'to do as I like' (of which the exaggerated form is the general wish to disobey), to go with big boys, to be a sea-captain, cowboy, or pirate. Now these, which with their like are all that lend charm to tobacco as an implement of boyhood, are all the clear outgrowths of the still earlier wish to 'run away' from home, so often seen in children of ten and less. This in turn is no innate tendency and must derive its impetus from somewhere. It does, and from just such sources as that which I first mentioned—an injudicious mother (or father) undertaking to be a fence between the child and its little bauble of flame. The cautious reaction was then secured toward flame-plus-mother; but the innate tendency to reach out toward flame (which in turn gets its energy from the flame stimulus direct) was not modified, as it would have been if the mother had *trusted* the simple truth that flame is hot. She wished to teach the child to avoid flame; what she did teach it was *to avoid her* (as being the impediment, which the flame itself ought to have been, to its innate tendency). This

THE WISH IN ETHICS 117

and similar misdirections on the parents' part soon produce a child that toddles off down the street in the aim of running away from home, and that later, in the desire to act grown-up and independent, assembles a gang of street gamins behind the barn to smoke cigarettes and gulp down poison from a whisky-bottle. For these children have been *taught* that fire does not burn. But all this must not be, and so the father finds himself 'forced' to get a rawhide whip; with which he adds fear to the already existing tendencies which make the child wish to act and to be 'grown-up' and forever away from parental restraints. When such motor settings are once established in a child, almost every object in the environment tends to stimulate them to action; and so the nervous paths of disobedience are amply energized. Tobacco is notably such an object.

All this is to say that in our boy whose parents have all along trusted the truth, the second step of which I spoke will be very simple, because the tendency or 'temptation' to the precocious use of tobacco (to be prematurely grown-up) was in this boy *not fed* from any considerable or regular source of energy. I believe that this is true. At least I have seen it to be true in several cases; that is to say, in one hundred per cent. of the fearlessly honest parents whom I have been able to discover. In these cases the children, so far from wishing to anticipate their departure from the parental roof, have evinced a wistful though unvoiced regret when the time for this came. It appears that where honesty prevails in the home, kindness, too, can be trusted to make her fixed abode. Nor have the children wished to dabble with tobacco. The case just considered illustrates the way in which, as Freud so emphatically declares, the difficulties of later life derive from suppressions and dissociations established in earliest childhood.

This second step, the resolution of a dilemma between courses of action, is not always so simple, and I wish to pass at once to a typical instance, which reveals, I believe, at one stroke how the will, the intellect, and the moral sense develop; the very pattern of the articulate integration of the soul. *

A young woman goes from a rural and pious home to a great city, there to earn her living. She

* The case of tobacco is not the one which I should like to call typical. Although not particularly apposite to my ultimate purpose, I chose it to illustrate a knotty and not uncommon special type of moral problem.

THE WISH IN ETHICS 119

makes the acquaintance of other young wage-earners, differently reared, who participate eagerly and thoughtlessly in the light-hearted amusements of the town. They go often to the theater. Our young woman has been taught at home that the theater is a place of all abominations, and from the conversation of her new acquaintances she judges that to some extent at least the parental opinion is well-founded. Shall she now adopt the practice of going to the theater? This is a legitimate and serious dilemma, because sound and insistent wishes make both for going and for not going. On the one hand are the proper curiosity of youth to see life, the love of companionship and gayety, the need for relaxation; on the other hand are the precepts of loving and trusted parents and of their religion, a sound prejudice against unbridled frivolity, and a normal shrinking from the moral contamination which the young woman sees is at work in her wage-earning friends.

We are fairly familiar with three ways in which persons behave when they meet such a dilemma. One way is to resist the present 'temptations,' which means to suppress the wish for companionship and pleasure, to renounce the 'tree of knowledge'; eventually to drift away from social connections, and into a warped, acidulous, and (as Freud finds) nervously diseased spinsterhood. A second way is to 'forget' (i.e., to suppress) the righteous precepts learned at home, to indulge unthinkingly in every 'pleasure' offered, to become the butterfly and the riotous pleasure-lover; which means eventually to drop into any and every form of abandonment, and to die a drunken prostitute. I state extreme cases; that is, cases in which the suppression persists. For as long as the suppression is there, the person is bound to move in the direction indicated. These two ways are equivalent in point of badness. In both cases the suppressed wishes inevitably burst forth in furtive side-channels of conduct. The ascetic 'hates' the "evils of this wicked world," despises and rankles over the frailties of his fellow-men, is seized by spasmodic impulses to kick over the traces himself, and is steadily obsessed by licentious thoughts. The abandoned pleasure-lover, similarly, has fits of 'remorse' and the haunting prick of 'conscience,' becomes maudlin and weepy at mention of 'home and mother,' asseverates with suspicious vehemence

THE WISH IN ETHICS

his having " always *tried* to do right," and calls for drink to allay his mental agony. When drunkest he babbles o' green fields, and blubbers, " See that my grave's kept green."

A third way is no better. It is the way of those who undertake to follow both of two conflicting courses; in the present instance, to observe both the church-going traditions of home and the morally relaxed habits of town. A person in this frame of mind will sometimes go to his clerical adviser with the proposal—" I'll go to all the services, take an active part in church work on Sunday, and contribute money, if you will agree that through the week I shall do anything I like." This is, of course, the path of 'compromise' in the most reprehensible sense of the word, and the direct route to all the vilest forms of hypocrisy. A progressive dissociation of the character is established, and the person becomes two persons, one pious and one pleasure-loving; an enigmatical character is produced, given to the most contradictory courses, restless, self-impeded, and at every point of social contact undependable. The case of Dr. Jekyll and Mr. Hyde is an extreme but not an overdrawn instance. This third way of meeting a dilemma resembles the other two in that dissociation takes place, and differs only in that neither branch of the character gains any considerable ascendency over the other. In the first two cases there is steady suppression of one set of tendencies, and a steady escape of these through furtive by-paths of thought and action; while in the third, each set of tendencies suffers alternate suppression. In none of the three cases is the victim able to do any one thing with his whole heart; a part of his strength has always to be spent in suppressing dissociated and antagonistic tendencies.

But there is a fourth way of meeting a dilemma, a way that involves integration and not dissociation nor yet suppression. Oddly enough it is not distinguished by superficial observers from the third way. It consists in a free play of *both* the involved sets of tendencies, whereby they *meet* each other, and a line of conduct emerges which is dictated by *both* sets of motives together, and which embodies all that was not downright antagonistic in the two. This sounds like compromise, whereas its mechanism is utterly different. And it were best called reconciliation or resolution. We return to our illustration of the young woman coming from

THE WISH IN ETHICS

a pious home to a great city. She is invited by a young man to go to a play. We have seen how in the interest of home piety she may suppress her natural curiosity and love of friends, and say "No"; or how in the latter interest she may suppress the home instructions, and say, "Yes." In either case only half of her has acted while the other half has been suppressed; and only half of her is active in going to the theater or, in the other case, participates in staying away. Suppose, however, that in this young woman her knowledge of the theater is not split into the two dissociated complexes of the deliciously pleasurable and the abhorrently wicked. She can view her invitation to the theater without either fascination or fear. Her knowledge, both direct and hearsay, as it accumulates, integrates around the central theme 'theater'; and her reactions toward this, the various appeals which this makes, *meet* one another, so that the theater's attractive and repulsive aspects, not being dissociated, work on one another directly, and this balanced interplay works itself out in a *discriminating* line of conduct. It is precisely like the case of fire which both pleases and yet burns the baby; who, if not artificially deterred, learns to handle fire discriminatingly. The young woman learns to avail herself of whatever is good in the theater and to avoid what is bad. The sanction is, here as before, the easily perceivable fact that the theater is partly good and partly bad. To the young man she probably replies, "I shall be delighted to go to the theater with you, but from what I read and hear I doubt if the play you mention would be altogether interesting to us. Shall we not choose another?" Now, this is not compromise; it is discrimination. It gives full play to all the individual's tendencies, and these are invariably to avoid evil, save when dissociation and its concomitant suppression have interfered with clear perception. Here nothing has been suppressed, and as the young woman follows out this line of action, her whole nature is actively participating. Her 'conscience,' too, is with her. And such a young woman will end neither as a careless butterfly nor as a grim ascetic. And it is to be noted that from this process of discrimination arises not merely sound moral choice in the individual, but sound moral development of the institution itself. The theater is not evolved into an instrument of civilization by either its undis-

THE WISH IN ETHICS

criminating devotees or its undiscriminating disparagers.

Here, as previously in the case of fire and of tobacco, we see that moral conduct is discriminating conduct; morality is wisdom. And as the will and the intellect are one, so they develop as one. We have seen that the element of conduct is a course of action toward the object or situation in the environment, and that such courses of action are embodied in motor attitudes of the individual toward the object or situation. Now since this Freudian point of view presents morals as nothing but the higher reaches of behavior, as in one continuous series, indeed, with natural history at large, it behooves us to inquire why and how suppression ever, rather than discrimination, comes to take place, and why suppression and dissociation are opposite to discrimination. Let us here consider the motor attitude of the average person toward mushrooms that he finds when out walking. I meet in a field near the edge of woods some clusters of low, small, light-brown mushrooms. These look like the edible *Agaricus campestris*, and I am inclined to eat some of them. But I have read that the very poisonous *Agaricus phalloides* in some of its seven varieties strongly resembles the *campestris*, and I have never learned the visible marks by which the two are to be distinguished. Therefore I am also inclined not to eat them. Here, then, I am in front of one object which stimulates in me two antagonistic courses of action—to sit down and eat, and to walk on, taking care not even to handle. I cannot do both, for they are opposed. And they are therefore dissociated, for it is probable that opposition is the one invariable source of dissociation. Whichever course of action I follow, the other is suppressed. But this latter gives evidences of itself, for if I walk on I find myself doing so lingeringly and casting my eyes back from time to time and wondering if these really are the poisonous ones; or if I sit down to eat some of them, I find myself only nibbling, every now and then rejecting a mouthful, and feeling a distinct tonus in my leg muscles urging me to be up and off. This is like the exquisitely logical position of one who, in throes of uncertainty whether to commit suicide, gulps down a tiny swallow of the poison. In short, my behavior toward mushrooms is thoroughly equivocal; one and the same visual stimulus excites in me two antagonistic responses,

THE WISH IN ETHICS

and I act *as if* * the mushrooms were *both* poisonous and not poisonous; that is, if I walk on, I am visibly impeded in doing so, and if I partake I cannot do so freely. This issue here involved would hardly be called a moral one, and yet the predicate 'wrong' would very naturally be applied to such an ambiguous attitude as the one described. We have so far one object responded to, two modes of response, their antagonism or dissociation, their interference and the partial suppression of each by the other.

But now let someone explain to me the visible marks of difference between the *Agaricus phalloides* and the *campestris*. At once my conduct is changed. Now on espying a cluster of light-brown mushrooms, I go directly up until I can see whether they are the *campestris* or the *phalloides*. And if they are the former, I sit down without compunction and eat my fill; if the latter, I resume my walk quite as if they did not exist. This is discrimination. The stimulus that formerly excited

---

* This is not a bad instance of the 'as if' relation, a relation which deserves more analysis than it has received. The employment of 'as if' and '*qua*' by philosophers gives the psychologist a certain clew as to the state of their cerebration.

two dissociated modes of response is now differentiated into two stimuli, each of which excites *one* of these modes. There is now no suppression because the other mode of response is not in the least degree stimulated. My conduct toward either mushroom is now *integral;* that is, the mechanism within me has taken one more step toward 'integration.' The dissociation of the two modes exists as before, but it is now harmless because the two will never again be excited by the one stimulus. In other words, it is not dissociated paths, but the simultaneous excitation of dissociated (i.e., antagonistic) paths by one stimulus that is harmful.

This makes clear, I trust, the relation between suppression, dissociation, and discrimination. My contention is that every moral failure and every moral triumph is precisely analogous to this case of the mushrooms. And we can now see how and why suppressions occur in this world of ours. It is through lack of knowledge. Our first contact with objects presents us with anomalies, contradictions, perplexities. Until further experience teaches us to discriminate further particulars within these objects, we shall be in some degree the victims of suppression, and our conduct will be to the same extent equivocal, immoral. A person who knows the theater only as 'the theater,' without internal distinction or nuance, observes that the most patternable persons support the institution without detriment to themselves, and on the other hand that the very dregs of society also go to 'the theater' and come away as from a bath in mud. For such a person, then, 'the theater' is good and it is bad; or it may present itself as 'delightful and yet sinful,' which is equally a flat contradiction in terms. And we have already considered the four possible ways of meeting the quandary—to go or not to go? Three of those ways showed suppression instead of discrimination, and they were bad. The fourth way was good because in it discrimination did away with suppression and produced coherent, integrated conduct. And lastly, if ill conduct arises through ignorance, the prevalence of such conduct is no mystery. In the bewildering turmoil which we witness where the sentiments and aims of individuals, of nations, and of races conflict with one another, we find an inexhaustible variety of contradictory appearances. These give rise to innumerable shortsighted and contradictory opinions both in the individual and in the collective mind.

And when these become crystallized in social convention, in the tenets and admonitions of the church, or in legislative enactments of the state, they constitute a bar to the progress of *discrimination*, an official ban (like primitive tabu) making for *suppression*. Thus it comes to pass that church and state often play in the adult's experience the rôle of shortsighted and injudicious parents. And these institutions, like the parent, find it advantageous to allege a moral sanction 'from above' which authorizes them to impose their will on society. A little insight into the actual workings of church and state shows how easily this allegation, untrue in the first instance, turns into an impudent piece of cajolery. It is truth and the ever-progressive discrimination of truth which alone conduce to moral conduct.

When all is said and done, the actual life of the will does consist of one long series of dilemmas, decisions to be made between two (or more) alternative courses of action: and the moral life consists in settling these issues 'rightly.' But then, we ask, what *is* ' right '? The answer indicated by the doctrine of the wish is simple and directly applicable in practice. Right is that conduct, at-

THE WISH IN ETHICS

tained through discrimination of the facts, which fulfils all of a man's wishes at once, suppressing none. The moral sanction is fact. The dilemma is always presented really to the intellect and the will together; which latter are in the last analysis one and inseparable. It is mental doubt as well as volitional indecision. It is not more the question, Shall I, or shall I not, eat this mushroom? than it is the question, Is this mushroom the edible or the poisonous one? And the moral failure is to act as if it were both edible and poisonous at once; which is just as clearly a confusion of the mind as it is of the will. The man who is secretly untrue to his friend is acting as if the latter at one time were, and at another time were not, his friend (this though the latter has not correspondingly altered): and this is an inconstancy or confusion of mind as well as of conduct. He is trying to keep his friend as friend (i.e., as an ally for purposes of mutual support) and yet trying to exploit his friend as victim (i.e., to the latter's undoing): and he is in the case of the fool who hopes to eat his pudding and yet to have it. Of course there are cute little arguments, propounded by Machiavelli and others, that the *maximum* advantage has to be squeezed out of any enterprise by judiciously-timed infidelities, betrayals, and so forth and so on. And these *all* hinge on the fallacy of ends: for a certain 'desirable end' a man will do this 'in itself objectionable' deed. But then when the end is obtained he is grieved to discover that it turns out to be *undesirable*, and he finds that it is rendered undesirable because of the very deed by which he attained it. This has been through all the ages the dying plaint of unprincipled and 'successful' men. It is only a question, once more, of being wise and observant enough to foresee that the taint attaching to the means is going to linger on and infect the end. The doctrine of the wish shows us that life is not lived *for ends*. Life is a process; it is a game to be played on the checkerboard of facts. Its motion is forward; yet its motive power comes not from in front (from 'ends') but from behind, from the wishes which are in ourselves. We shall play the game rightly if, instead of so painfully scrutinizing and trying to suppress our wishes, we turn about and lucidly discriminate the facts.

That is ethics 'from below.' The ethics 'from above' are a very different story. There Someone exhorts or obliges *us* to suppress our wishes, and

THE WISH IN ETHICS 133

if we observe Someone a bit carefully we shall all too often find that he generously busies *himself* with suppressing the facts. Ethics from above come indeed from above, from the man or the institution 'higher up.' And for this there is a very frail and human reason, which no one need go very far to discover. According to the ethics from below, the unassuming ethics of the dust, facts are the sole moral sanction: and facts impose the most inexorable moral penalties.

CHAPTER IV

SOME BROADER ASPECTS OF THE FREUDIAN ETHICS

THE ethical considerations which I have endeavored to present, and which I venture to think are a direct logical deduction from Freud's keen observations on the human mind, are not wholly out of touch with earlier thought in the ethical field. I believe, however, that the formula which we have now arrived at, for it is so far a formula rather than a completed system, is, as compared with the previous ethical formulations to which it is most akin, more clear, exact, and concrete. It is a definite description of what moral conduct is, and therefore by the same token is a practical guide, a precept, for one who desires to meet the dilemmas of life in a moral way. Thus our present formula,—to avoid the suppression of any reaction tendency by a more complete discrimination of the elements in the situation to be reacted upon, to

ASPECTS OF FREUDIAN ETHICS 135

resolve every situation rather than to do violence to it by a summary Yes or No,—is unmistakably reminiscent of that 'mean' of conduct which Aristotle praised so highly. Yet I do not see that Aristotle has shown us the clear and important distinction between the middle course of compromise, in its worst sense, and the middle course of rational discrimination. Indeed, Aristotle's commendation of the 'mean' is dangerously near being a general counsel of lukewarmness; although doubtless he did not intend it to be that. The same is to be said of many other similar utterances, such as Dante's condemnation of excess and Ruskin's praise of 'temperance.' They are in some sense true, but are too abstract to be a wholly feasible practical guide. If Dante is right, that every vice is a virtue carried to an unlawful extreme, it is still necessary for us to know what virtue is and what that quantity of it is which becomes unlawful.

A closer affinity exists, as the reader will have already noticed, between our ethical formula and the three steps of the Hegelian dialectic. Our case of the woman urged by opposing views and desires regarding the theater, and finally reconciling these by a process of discrimination, could be cited by

Hegel as a clear case of thesis, antithesis, and synthesis. Hegel is at the moment so greatly out of fashion that one hesitates to cast a single pebble; indeed, I would rather take the opportunity to say that, as it seems to me, Hegel is almost the only philosopher who has dealt at all responsibly with the problem of error. And anyone is very welcome to undertake to prove that our dilemma of opposing motives and its resolution is only an instance of the three movements in the dialectic. Yet I must insist that one gains a cleaner psychological analysis and a more usable, not to say a sounder, understanding of synthesis and resolution, by studying human conduct from the Freudian rather than the Hegelian point of view. Hegel leads one to suppose (though how fully he intended to do so I cannot say) that opposites *are* reconciled in the final synthesis; that, to revert to our last illustration, the good and the evil of the theater are seen to be somehow actually reconciled and merged if one only views the theater comprehensively enough. This is, however, precisely what they are not: the good and the evil of the theater remain everlastingly arrayed against each other. And for this very reason they can be everlastingly discriminated. Hegel seems to dissolve evil, and to turn contradiction and negation into mere 'appearance,' unreality. He does not appreciate, as Freud does, their so very potent reality. On the other hand, curiously enough, the Hegelian argument has given rise to the practical belief that opposition and conflict are desirable, are to be encouraged and promoted—because they will eventually emerge in a triumphant 'synthesis.' Thus it is argued that in parliament and convention it is better that there should be several parties and factions, each represented by men who act solely in the interests of the party or faction, than that all members should seek to view impartially all of the various considerations to be met, and all work directly for their just reconciliation. This is to say that conflict is better than cooperation. Such a doctrine may seem too strange to be credible, and yet I think it will be found to be a practical maxim of the day. Its widespread acceptance accounts for the disappearance of what was once called statesmanship from the government of several great countries. This fatal doctrine has its root in the conviction (peculiarly Hegelian, I believe) that opposition is the *very condition* not merely of progress, but even of process. Nothing takes place without conflict, and hence, to adduce an exact parallel, friction is the cause of motion. And here it is worth noting that the Hegelian reality, the 'Absolute,' is absolutely static. Since conflict is unreal, so motion must also be unreal. Applied to human behavior, this doctrine would assert that that person is nearest to synthesized activity whose native tendencies are the most completely dissociated and antagonistic. In short, Hegel and his school have altogether lost sight of harmony in process. Now it is one thing to say that conflict is desirable because it leads to a resolution, and a very different to say that resolution is desirable because it does away with conflict. The Hegelian emphasis is a downright fallacy. And thus while the Freudian formula moves in three steps which are to some extent analogous with the three phases of thesis, antithesis, and synthesis, it is nevertheless a very different analysis of the moral problem. The similarity is in fact superficial.

A far more interesting and indeed a remarkable point of contact between the view here outlined and the history of ethics is to be found in the

Socratic and Platonic conception of the will. In the 'Gorgias' (468) Socrates says: "We will to do that which conduces to our good, and if the act is not conducive to our good we do not will it; for we will, as you say, that which is our good, but that which is neither good nor evil, or simply evil, we do not will." And again, Socrates asks Polus: "But does he [any man] do what he wills if he does what is evil? Why do you not answer?" Pol. "Well, I suppose he does not." And again, in the "Protagoras" (358) we read: "Then you agree, I [Socrates] said, that the pleasant is the good, and the painful evil. . . . Then, I said, if the pleasant is the good, nobody does anything under the idea or conviction that some other thing would be better and is also attainable, when he might do the better. And this inferiority of a man to himself is merely ignorance, as the superiority of a man to himself is wisdom. . . . Then, I said, no man voluntarily pursues evil, or that which he thinks to be evil. To prefer evil to good is not in human nature; and when a man is compelled to choose one of two evils, no one will choose the greater when he might have the less."

The argument seems to be that we *do* things which are not conducive to our good, but we do not *will* them. And if we do them it is through ignorance, and of course we are not free to will that which our ignorance hides from us. The more psychological distinction between will and free-will is not drawn, and the upshot of the argument is that none but the wise man is free to will. Wisdom and virtue are one, and only the wise and virtuous man is free.

Aristotle, with a characteristic touch, hastened to blur this clear-cut picture by declaring that the evil man is equally free to will his evil; thus entirely disposing of the doctrine that wisdom and virtue are the same, and are essential to freedom. And the Socratic-Platonic doctrine has remained comparatively without influence ever since. Thomas Aquinas upheld it, but nevertheless the subsequent history of ethics and psychology shows a steady degradation of this high-minded doctrine; it giving way to the dogma that moral 'responsibility' demands a 'contingency' in human action, to the dogma of 'absolute fiat,' and so forth. Perhaps it is that no philosopher since Thomas has had a sufficient acquaintance with both virtue and wisdom to recognize their identity; or perhaps the so-called science of psychology developed a system of vagaries in which the earlier truth could find no place. In any case the Socratic doctrine of the identity of wisdom, virtue, and freedom has been left, as if it were a romantic dream, too exalted and unreal for either ecclesiastical or academic ethics to take hold of.

Now the Freudian ethics is a literal and concrete justification of the Socratic teaching. We have seen throughout that truth is the sole moral sanction, and that the discrimination of hitherto unrealized facts is the one way out of every moral dilemma. This is precisely to say that virtue is wisdom. Freud gives the subject a more concrete psychological analysis than did Socrates or Plato; and he proves the doctrine to hold in the special case. And as regards freedom, Freud's confirmation is even more remarkable. We have seen that the opposite of discrimination is suppression, the condition in which a person in the face of a given situation is stimulated to two (or more) antagonistic courses of action, so that whichever course he pursues, the antagonistic innervations prompting to the other course constantly impede him; as I showed especially in the instance of the mushrooms. Such a person is not *free* to take any of the courses, but in every case is hampered and held back by his own opposed inclinations. This is indeed the very serfdom of the will. And freedom, like virtue, comes through discrimination, i.e., wisdom. The person in whom there are no suppressions, in whom the process of discrimination and integration has gone on successfully, throws his whole force into whatever he does; he does it without constraint. This person has 'free-will.' And so for Freud, as for Socrates, wisdom, virtue, and freedom are all one condition of the soul. Freud has shown how the soul that fails to attain this condition, that fails to develop through progressive integrations, is strikingly inhibited, repressed, and unfree; and in his psychiatrical and other volumes has copiously illustrated the variety of ways in which such failures occur. And it is rather interesting to note that in many of these cases one is at first puzzled whether to describe the difficulty as nervous malady, mental inhibition, or moral perversity: a perplexing circumstance until one realizes that all three pertain to one and the same genus—suppression.

ASPECTS OF FREUDIAN ETHICS 143

The Socratic doctrine is of such cardinal importance that it is worth while to consider two of the apparent objections to it. For it is often plausibly alleged that on the one hand many thoroughly virtuous persons are yet unwise and ill of soul, while on the other hand many wicked persons are perfectly healthy and most desperately cunning. Indeed, so proverbial is this that Mephistopheles, the archfiend, is always represented as a supreme intellect. As to the first of these arguments, it is of course admitted that rain and lightning fall on the just and the unjust alike; so that the virtuous person is liable indeed to physical illness and lingering forms of death. But all the curious inadvertencies and stupidities of the so-called virtuous, and all their ailments which by any possibility can be called mental, are found, when they are analyzed and understood, to be quite as much departures from virtue, in the broader sense of the term, as they are departures from health or wisdom. Freud has given us a thousand classical examples, to which Alfred Adler has added further cases, which show how oblique and unhallowed motives are habitually suppressed (*not* victoriously overcome by discrimination) in order to produce the *appearance* of virtue, and how just these suppressions work havoc with every aspect of mental integrity. It is thus the *apparently* most virtuous who are the *most* often afflicted with mental disabilities of one sort and another. It is not to be wondered at that the popular misapprehension has arisen. But the genuinely virtuous, those who have integrated away every suppression, are also the genuinely healthy of mind. And let no one think of his poor dear friends, A., B., and C., as paragons of virtue yet afflicted with morbid anxiety, forgetfulness, motor incoördinations, bad dreams, or hallucinations, until he has studied Freud's cases and learned to read the sort of subconscious wishes that lurk beneath a virtue so extreme and so bedridden. Moreover, the inconveniences consequent on suppression are often of a sort that seems to be entirely physical—migraine, lameness, etc.; and herein, perhaps, lies whatever is true in a certain half-truth that has been utilized by Christian Science.

Secondly, in regard to those who are wicked and yet seem to be both healthy and shrewd, it is to be admitted at once that such persons sometimes have few internal suppressions. They have developed *so far* fairly healthily, and they have largely avoided suppressions by dint of a studied inattention to the disagreeable and a frank pursuit of whatever pleases them regardless of consequences. The downright wicked person sometimes has the *virtue* of not being a hypocrite. But all this is, as I said, regardless of consequences. And the consequences soon appear, so that the latter end of the wicked presents a picture of abject mental inadequacy, the cruelest suppressions, and presently of mental disease. We often think of the wicked as supremely young, just taken in some act of dashing highwaymanship, and while envying them their youthful vigor we forget that they are true cases of arrested development. In short, the picture we make to ourselves is of the brief heyday of wickedness, and we fail to see that this very wickedness reveals a now arrested integration, and that the next phase will be a fearful display of suppressions, anxieties, and mental incapacity (and all this apart from any artificial penalties which the wickedness may incur). An important circumstance which often hides from us the fact that wisdom and virtue are in principle one, and that principle the progressive lifelong integration of experience, is that the earlier steps of integration concern merely the child's successful navigation of his immediate tangible surroundings. The recession of the stimulus has as yet not proceeded very far. As the stimulus recedes further, that is, as the integration of experience continues, the things with which the youth learns how to deal are less and less tangible objects, but are rather aspects, situations, and the like. Then develop integrated modes of behavior toward more comprehensive aspects, such as science, business, and society at large; while the highest stages of integration produce the most comprehensive courses of action, and these are inevitably of the sort which we call moral. In moral conduct the stimulus has receded the farthest and such conduct is behavior toward the most *universal* entities, toward truth, honor, virtue, and the like. And one further stage is possible, the religious. Thus we say that at first the child is developing its body, then its practical intelligence, then its theoretical mind, then its moral and finally its religious 'nature.' So that if integration ceases at a certain point, we may see the phenomenon of a fairly sound body and mind, lacking both morals and religion.

Nevertheless I am careful to say only '*fairly sound.*' For in point of fact it appears that the process which will definitely stop the integration at any one of its later stages generally commences very early in the child's life, perhaps in the cradle. And if the moral nature is never to be developed, certain warps and twists can generally be found in the already existing mind, which show why its future growth is to be thus limited. The Mephistopheles legend, of a very wicked man yet thoroughly master of himself and sound in body and mind, is about as untruthful a picture as mythology affords.* It may be here hinted that at the present stage of 'western civilization' the moral, and the higher stages of mental, integration appear most often to shatter on a very prevalent malformation of what may be called the 'ego complex.' But to develop this theme further would be beyond our present scope.†

Thus for the Freudian view which I have endeavored to outline morality is the most inclusive knowledge. Ethics is solely a question, as Epic-

* It is interesting to note the prevailing cynicism of the societies and epochs in which this tradition has flourished.
† Cf. Alfred Adler: "Ueber den nervösen Charakter." Bergman, Wiesbaden, 1912.

tetus so long ago said, of "dealing wisely with the phenomena of existence." In a way, indeed, this has been the main contention of all practical moralists. What is new is that Freud shows what in the concrete case the mental mechanism of wise dealing is. It is the establishment through discrimination of consistent and not contradictory (mutually suppressive) courses of action toward phenomena. The moral sanction lies always in facts presented by the phenomena; morality in the discrimination of those facts.

This is, of course, an ethic 'from below.' For such a view morals evolve and develop; they grow, and are a part of the general growth and evolution of the universe. This is in sharp contrast with a considerable portion of academic ethics, where in one form or another we find the intimation that moral ideals are something imposed 'from above'; the moral sanction is somehow supermundane. And these academic discussions themselves of ethics hang suspended in the air, and seem unable to establish connection with the world in which we live. Thus 'the good,' for an instance, is in many modern (and for that matter ancient) discussions the subject-matter of ethics, but it appears that

ASPECTS OF FREUDIAN ETHICS 149

this ' good ' can be neither defined nor pointed out, and surely until this pivotal entity can be somehow located among the concrete phenomena of existence, the ethical fabric that rests thereon is merely a systematic jargon. Or again, we find the word ' value ' as representing the cardinal concept of systematic ethics. It is a popular word just now, and is the theme of no end of current philosophic vagarizing. But this word, too, despite its seemingly more definite psychological meaning, retains a deal of the same abstract and unseizable quality. It is merely a sort of psychological synonym for ' the good.'

In nearly all these philosophic discussions of ethics one has somehow the haunting sense of a wrongness of direction. Virtue is somehow imposed from above, it is descending upon us. And the unfortunate part of this is that it has to descend very low indeed before it reaches us; and when there, it has lost the buoyancy wherewith to lift us up. Also this academic misapprehension may be seen reflected in the practical sphere. We hear everywhere of bringing this and that good thing down to the unfortunate and the debased, and then of ' *adapting* ' it to the taste and comprehension of these same unfortunate and debased. Thus at the present moment a so-called evangelist who is touring the country is accounted thoroughly successful in "bringing the gospel to the masses"; and his method is to couch his message in language that would make a cowboy blush. He has reached the masses indeed, and gone lower than the masses; but has not the 'gospel' become somewhat unrecognizably transformed during this descent? It seems to me a palpable fact that every form of philanthropy and 'social service' to-day is more or less infected with this fallacy. The idea is everywhere to bring the good *down*, in the false hope that this will somehow lift the masses up. But why shall anything strive upwards, when all that is high is bidden to descend? And is it not a striking and ominous fact that to-day the word 'aspire' is never heard?

These egregious ethics of the air have produced other tangible and all-pervading consequences. Since 'ethics' is such a floating vapor, many sober-minded persons conclude, and not illogically, that it is quite apart from the practical conduct of life. And they lead their lives accordingly. Thus the Teutonic races, in their rigorous fashion, have

ASPECTS OF FREUDIAN ETHICS 151

codified this conclusion. Ethics, they explicitly say, have no part to play in politics and statecraft; these are a science and they deal solely with realities. This science is '*Realpolitik*,' the Politics of Reality. The effect of such a doctrine when put in practice is now being written on the pages of the world's history in letters so large that even he who runs must read. And similarly, the world over, it tends to be held by high and low that the 'scientific' attitude *supersedes* the ethical. The ethics of the air are indeed effete.

But set against all this, and as different from it as the day from night, are the ethics of the dust. It presents mind itself as an evolution, and morals as one of the higher stages of this process. Here we have man, as 'real' and as 'scientific' as you please, growing upwards. (And I insist that the direction is somehow right.) He who does not see the *real* sanction of morality, that morality is a stage of wisdom and a step higher than 'science,' is merely shortsighted. And the facts can safely be trusted to impress in due time their lesson, to drive us on to morals. On such an ethics it seems to me that Freud's discovery of the 'wish,' the articulate unit of mind and character, casts considerable light. Much remains to be learned, but in this learning it may be that the suppression-discrimination formula for wishes, which we have been studying, will serve somewhat as a talisman.

SUPPLEMENT

RESPONSE AND COGNITION *

I. THE SPECIFIC-RESPONSE RELATION

THE novelty exhibited by things at the moment of their synthesis into an organized whole has been frequently commented on. Such moments may seem to be 'critical,' as when two gases condense into a liquid and the phenomena exhibited by gases are replaced by those characteristic of fluids; or there may be less appearance of discontinuity, as when a solid is slowly dissolved in a liquid and the latter as slowly acquires new properties. In either case, separate entities have been organized into a new whole, and their former action as independent parts is now combined in the action of the whole. And while it is obvious that the whole is nothing more than the parts as thus organized, and that the properties of the whole are nothing more than

* Reprinted from *The Journal of Philosophy, Psychology, and Scientific Methods,* Vol. XII, Nos. 14 and 15, July 8 and July 22, 1915.

the properties of the parts now acting in coöperation, it is nevertheless true that the whole now does things which the isolated parts never did or could do. New phenomena, new laws and functions have been developed.

Most of us believe that the appearance of life was such a critical moment in the evolution of the universe: that life came into existence when some, perhaps a specific, sort of chemical process was set up under such conditions as maintained it around a general point of equilibrium. The result was undoubtedly novel; and more novelties were to come. Living substance was to acquire a protective envelope, to become irritable, conductive, and contractile, to develop specific irritability to many stimuli, to get the power of locomotion, and much else. Now in the course of this further evolution, there is a critical point which is worthy of notice. It is the point where the irritable, contractile, and conductive tissues develop systematic relations which enable them to function as an integral whole. Here, too, novelty ensues.

How 'critical' this point is, how sudden and well-defined, or, on the other hand, how gradual, cannot as yet be told. The integrative process in the nervous system, as Sherrington so well calls it, has not, even yet, been observed in sufficient detail. But this is of secondary importance; and the result of the process we do know definitely. This is, that the phenomena evinced by the integrated organism are no longer merely the excitation of nerve or the twitching of muscle, nor yet the play merely of reflexes touched off by stimuli. These are all present and essential to the phenomena in question, but they are merely components now, for they have been integrated. And this integration of reflex arcs, with all that they involve, into a state of systematic interdependence has produced something that is not merely reflex action. The biological sciences have long recognized this new and further thing, and called it 'behavior.'

Of recent years, many of the workers in animal psychology have been coming to call this the science of behavior, and have been dwelling less and less on the subject of animal 'consciousness.' They do not doubt, any of them, that at least the higher animals are 'conscious'; but they find that nothing but the behavior of animals is susceptible of scientific observation. Furthermore, several students in the human field have come to the same conclusion—that not the 'consciousness,' but the behavior of one's fellow-men, and that alone, is open to investigation. Several volumes have been put forth which even undertake to construe human psychology entirely in terms of behavior. It is obvious that this is an unstable condition in which the science now finds itself. We cannot continue thus, each man proclaiming his own unquestionable gift of 'consciousness,' but denying that either his fellowmen or the animals evince the slightest indication of such a faculty. Now I believe that a somewhat closer definition of 'behavior' will show it to involve a hitherto unnoticed feature of novelty, which will throw light on this matter.

Precisely how does this new thing, 'behavior,' differ, after all, from mere reflex action? Cannot each least quiver of each least muscle fiber be wholly explained as a result of a stimulus impinging on some sense-organ, and setting up an impulse which travels along definite nerves with definite connections, and comes out finally at a definite muscle having a certain tonus, etc., all of which is merely reflex action? Yes, exactly *each least* component can be so explained, for that is just what, and all that, it is. But it is the coördinated totality

RESPONSE AND COGNITION 157

of these least components which *cannot* be described in such terms, nor indeed in terms resembling these. For such neural and reflex terms fail to seize that integration factor which has now transformed reflex action into something else, i.e., behavior. We require, then, an exact definition of behavior.

But before proceeding to this definition we shall probably find useful an illustration from another science, which was once in the same unstable state of transition as psychology is now. In physics a theory of causation once prevailed, which tried to describe causal process in terms of successive 'states,' the 'state' of a body at one moment being the *cause* of its 'state' and position at the next. Thus the course of a falling body was described as a series of states (a, b, c, d, etc.), each one of which was the effect of the state preceding, and cause of the one next following. This may be designated as the 'bead theory' of causation. Inasmuch, however, as nothing could be observed about one of these 'states' which would show why the next 'state' must necessarily follow, or, in other words, since the closest inspection of 'states' gave no clew toward explaining the course or even the continuance of the process, an unobservable impetus (*vis viva*, *Anstoss*, 'force') was postulated This hidden impetus was said to be the ultimate secret of physical causation. But, alas, a secret! For it remained, just as the 'consciousness' of one's fellow-man remains to-day in psychology,* utterly refractory to further investigation. Now 'myth' is the accepted term to apply to an entity which is believed in, but which eludes empirical inquiry. This mythical *vis viva* has now, in good part owing to the efforts of Kirchhoff and Hertz, been rejected, and, what is more important, with it has gone the bead theory itself. It is not the 'previous state' of the falling body which causes it to fall, but the earth's mass. And it is not in the 'previous state' but in laws that explanation resides, and no laws for falling bodies or for any other process could, on the terms of the bead theory, be extracted from the phenomena. But laws were easily found for physical processes, if the observer persuaded himself to make the simple

---

* The transition here in question has been admirably stated, from a slightly different point of view, by W. P. Montague, in "The Relational Theory of Consciousness and its Realistic Implications"; in this *Journal*, Vol. III, pp. 309-316.

inquiry, *What* are the objects *doing?* * Now the falling body is not merely moving downwards past the successive divisions of a meter-stick which I have placed beside it (which is all that the bead theory would have us consider), nor is it essentially moving toward the floor which, since a floor happens to be there, it will presently strike. The body is *essentially* moving toward the center of the earth, and these other objects could be removed without altering the influence of gravity. In short, the fall of a body is adequately described as a function of its mass, of the earth's mass, and of the distance between the centers of the two. And the *function* is *constant*, is that which in change remains unchanged (in the case cited it is a constant acceleration). The physical sciences, of course, have now explicitly adopted this function theory of causation.† Every physical law is in the last analysis the statement of a constant function between one process or thing and some other process or thing. This abandonment of the bead theory in

* That the answer to this question explains also *why* they do it, is an important point, but one with which we are not now concerned.

† Cf. E. Cassirer, " Substanzbegriff und Funktionsbegriff," Berlin, 1910. The sciences have implicitly used this method from the very beginning.

favor of the function theory requires, at the first, some breadth and some bravery of vision.

Now psychology is at the present moment addicted to the bead theory, and I believe that this is responsible for the dispute about 'consciousness' *versus* behavior. Our disinclination to follow the physical sciences, to adopt the functional view in place of the bead theory, has hindered us from defining accurately what behavior is, and this has prevented us from recognizing a remarkable novelty which is involved in behavior, and which is the result of reflex action becoming organized.

We are prone, even the 'behaviorists' among us, to think of behavior as somehow consisting of reflex activities. Quite true, so far as it goes. So, too, coral reefs in the last analysis consist of positive and negative ions, but the biologist, geographer, or sea-captain would miss his point if he conceived them in any such terms. Yet we are doing the very same thing when we conceive the behavior of a man or animal in the unintegrated terms of neural process; which means, agreeably to the bead theory, the impinging of stimulus on sense-organ, the propagation of ionization waves along a fiber, their spread among various other fibers, their combining

RESPONSE AND COGNITION 161

with other similar waves, and eventually causing the lowered or heightened tonus of muscle. All this is happening. But our account has overlooked the most essential thing of all—the *organization* of these processes.

If now we pitch the misleading bead theory straight overboard, and put our microscope back into its case, we shall be free to look at our behaving organism (man, animal, or plant), and to propound the only pertinent, scientific question— *What* is this organism *doing?* All agree that empirical study will elicit the answer to this question, and in the end the complete answer.

What, then, *is* it doing? Well, the plant is being hit by the sun's rays and is turning its leaves until they all lie exactly at right angles to the direction of these rays: the stentor, having swum into a region of CO_2, is backing off, turning on its axis, and striking out in a new direction: the hen has got a retinal image of a hawk and she is clucking to her brood—shoot the hawk or remove the brood and she stops clucking, for she is reacting to neither one nor the other, but to a situation in which both are involved: the man is walking past my window; no, I am wrong, it is not past my window that he is walking; it is *to* the theater; or am I wrong again? Perhaps the man is a journalist, and not the theater, nor yet the play, but the 'society write-up' it is to which the creature's movements are adjusted; further investigation is needed. This last instance is important, for the man 'walking past my window' is generally doing so in no more pertinent a sense than does the dead leaf fall to the ground 'past my window.' Both are *doing* something else. Herein the folly of the bead theory becomes clear. This theory says that in order to understand the man's actions, as he walks by, we must consider his successive 'states,' for each one is the cause of each succeeding one. And if we follow the theory faithfully, it leads us back to the successive 'states' of each component process, and ever back, till we arrive at the flow of ions in neuro-muscular tissue; in which disintegrating process the *man* with which he started is completely dissolved and lost.* But now the functional view, moving in

* Philosophers have justly denounced this view, but in their reaction have hit on another, the teleological, which is unfortunately no truer to the facts, as I shall show further on. It is singular that philosophy at large, having seen the inadequacy of the bead theory, should have retained it; retained it, that is, for the 'mechanical realm'; and this even after the mechanists had abandoned it.

precisely the opposite direction, admonishes us to keep the man whole (if it is *behavior* that we are studying) and to study his movements until we have discovered *exactly what* he is doing, that is, until we have found that object, situation, process (or perhaps merely that relation) of which his behavior is a *constant function*. The analysis of this behavior, as thus exactly described, will come in later; but it in turn will be carried on in the same spirit—i.e., of discovering always and solely *functions*. The movements of a plant, animal, or man are always a constant function of something, or a combination of such constant functions, and these —the movements, the functions, and the things of which the movements are a function—are always open to empirical investigation.

As a matter of fact the biologists and the behaviorists are doing just this thing—discovering constant functions. They are describing the motions of plant leaves as a function of the direction of the sun's rays, and are doing the same for all the aspects of animal behavior as well. They have done this for a long time. And there is nothing 'novel' in behavior as so described. My point is, firstly, that while the behaviorists are indeed doing this, which is just the right thing, they do not realize the significance of that which they are doing. And this is because, secondly, they are not aware of the remarkable novelty which behavior, considered just as they are considering it, does in fact involve.

An exact definition of behavior will reveal this. Let us go about this definition. *Behavior is*, firstly, *a process of release.* The energy with which plants and animals move ('behave') is not derived from the stimulus, but is physiologically stored energy previously accumulated by processes of assimilation. The stimulus simply touches off this energy.

Secondly, *behavior is not a function of the immediate stimulus.* There are cases, it is true, in which behavior is a function, though even here not a very simple function, of the stimulus. These are cases of behavior in its lower stages of development, where it is just emerging from the direct reflex process. They demonstrate the *continuity* of evolution at this point—a most important fact. But as behavior evolves, any correlation between it and the stimuli which are immediately affecting the organism becomes increasingly remote, so that even in fairly simple cases it can no longer be demonstrated. This fact, that the immediate stimulus recedes in importance, is the interesting point about the integration of reflexes. It has been widely recognized in psychology; perhaps most conspicuously by Spencer, who generally refers to it under the term 'higher correspondence.' One will see in what relatively early stages of integration the immediate stimulus is thus lost sight of, if one considers how even the ' retinal image ' (to say nothing of the distant object which casts that image) is not, in an exact sense, the actual physiological stimulus; yet the organism 'behaves' with regard only to the distant object. Since, then, behavior is not essentially a function of immediate stimulus, this latter cannot enter into a definition of behavior.

But on the other hand, thirdly, behavior *remains a function of some object, process, or aspect of the objective environment* (including, in rare cases, the internal vegetative organs; which are still, however, 'objective'). And this is our crucial point. Not quite adequately realized by the behaviorists, it is *terra totaliter incognita* to the subjectivists. And the proposition negates their whole gospel, including especially the notion of 'consciousness.'

I shall revert to this. Here we need only note that the behaving organism, whether plant, fellow-man, or one's own self, is always doing something, and the fairly *accurate description* of this activity will invariably reveal a law (or laws) whereby this activity is shown to be a constant function of some aspect of the objective world. One has here the same task as in any other strictly physical science. In both cases some accuracy is needed, and in both alike this accuracy can generally be advanced by more exhaustive observation. Thus it is inaccurate to say that a river flows toward the sea, since it meanders about in all directions; while it is fairly accurate to describe it as always flowing toward the next lower level of the earth's surface, and this is a law describing flow as a constant function of the earth's crust and the position of the earth's center. The test is, of course, whether this or that could be removed *without changing* the river's course: the 'sea' could be removed, the 'next lower level' could not. So in behavior, the flock of birds is not, with any accuracy, flying over the green field; it is, more essentially, flying southwards; but even this is only a rough approximation to a law of migration. In all events the flock of birds is doing something, and the sole question which we need ever ask is, "What is it doing?" I have elsewhere explained how the same question, and it alone, is applicable to *one's own* behavior (voluntary or other).*

Now I believe that the foregoing three propositions yield a definition of behavior. It would run: *Behavior is any process of release which is a function of factors external to the mechanism released.*

But why 'any' process when it is well known that behavior is a phenomenon found in none but living organisms? Precisely because behavior as thus defined is in fact a striking novelty, which does not, so far as I am able to ascertain, occur anywhere in the evolutionary series prior to the appearance of organized response. This point is somewhat later, too, than that at which life appears. In the ordinary inorganic case of released energy, the process, once touched off, proceeds solely according to factors internal to the mechanism released. When a match is touched to gunpowder the explosion is a function of nothing but the amount, quality, arrangement, etc., of the

* Cf. my "Concept of Consciousness." Geo. Allen and Macmillan, 1914. Pp. 287 *et seq*.

powder. The beginning of the process is a function of the moment of firing; but that is all. When, on the other hand, an organism with integrated nervous system is stimulated, the organism, by virtue of internal energy released, proceeds to do something of which the strict scientific description can only be that it is a constant function of some feature of the environment; and this latter is by no means necessarily the stimulus itself. The organism responds specifically to something outside,* just as the falling body moves specifically toward the earth's center. This fact offers no opening for the introduction here of 'subjective' categories: the investigator continues to ask, merely, What is the organism doing? The answer will be in strictly objective terms. It cannot be said that the ordinary release process is a function of the temperature, moisture, etc., of the surrounding air, for it is in fact a function of these only in so far as they penetrate and become internal to the released mechanism. In behavior, on the other hand, there is a genuine 'objective reference' to the invironment which is not found, so far as I can learn,

* The above is that stricter definition of 'specific response' which I have previously said ("The New Realism," 1912, p. 355) that I hoped some day to be able to give.

in the inorganic, or in the organic world prior to integrated reflex response. This is the novelty which characterizes behavior. And here, if anywhere, evolution turned a corner.

In the second place, it may be noted that the definition neither excludes nor yet makes essential the case of the immediate stimulus being the object of which the behavior is a constant function. This often happens, and is characteristic of the simpler instances where behavior is only beginning to be differentiated from plain reflex action. Evolution is of course not discontinuous, and the development from reflex action to highly organized behavior is one in which the correlation between stimulus and organism becomes less and less direct, while that between the organism and the object of response becomes more and more prominent. Plain reflex action is a function of the stimulus and of factors internal to the neuro-muscular arc. Then presently one finds reflex movements that are due, as one must (with Sherrington) agree, to 'so-to-say stored stimuli'; since the immediate stimulus does not account for the reflex movement. It is here that behavior begins, and precisely here that the 'bead theory' would lead us astray. The response in question is a response to a past event, it is describable only in terms of (as a function of) this past event; while the bead theory would let us look only to the present condition of neuro-muscular tissue, the 'so-to-say stored stimuli.' These are of course an integral part of the causal process, but not the more enlightening part; just as the measurements of the velocity of a body at successive moments are an integral part of its fall to earth, while if we considered *nothing* but these, we should never arrive at the true law of fall—a constant acceleration toward the earth's center. Or it is again as if, when one had photographed the spectrum of a newly-discovered earth, one were misled by the bead theory into considering the result as 'merely light and dark parallel lines on a gelatine negative.' It is this, indeed, but it is also an interesting combination of metallic spectra. Or, again, the camera photographs a motor-car race, and the sensitive plate is affected a millionth of a second later than that in which the phase photographed occurred. By the time the print is obtained the race is long since over. The bead theory then says: This is only a black-and-white mottled slip of paper, it is no function of the racing motors. It is in just this

RESPONSE AND COGNITION 171

way that in studying behavior we think that the only scientific view of it must be in terms of ionized nerve and twitching muscle. Is it any wonder, then, that having ignored the *objective functional reference of behavior*, we are led into the superstition of 'ideas' in the 'sensorium' which have an 'objective reference' to the environment?

If now the behaviorist will bear in mind that he is scientifically justified in asking broadly, What is the organism doing?, he will discover that it is set to act as a constant function of some aspect of the environment, and he will find this to be the scientific description of the phenomenon he is studying. Then with this accurate description as a basis, he can proceed to analyze it into its reflex components and the relations by which they have been organized into behavior.

II. COGNITION AS RESPONSE

We have now a compact and, as I believe, a rather precise definition of behavior or, as it might be called, the relation of specific response. And we are in a position to compare it with the cognitive relation, the relation between the 'psychological subject and its object of consciousness.' Our aim would be to see how far those phenomena which we ordinarily attribute to 'consciousness' may be intrinsically involved by this strictly objective and scientifically observable behavior.

Firstly, as to the object cognized, the 'content of consciousness.' It is obvious that the object of which an organism's behavior is a constant function corresponds with singular closeness to the object of which an organism is aware, or of which it is conscious. When one is conscious of a thing, one's movements are adjusted to it, and to precisely those features of it of which one is conscious. The two domains are conterminous. It is certain, too, that it is not generally the stimulus to which one is adjusted, or of which one is conscious: as such classic discussions as those about the inverted retinal image and single vision (from binocular stimulation) have shown us. Even when one is conscious of things that are not there, as in hallucination, one's body is adjusted to them as if they were there; and it behaves accordingly.* In some

* I have elsewhere tried to show (in the fifth essay of "The New Realism") that every type of subjective error has an analogue in the strictly physical realm.

sense or other they are there; as in some sense there are objects in mirrored space. Of course the objects of one's consciousness, and of one's motor adjustments, may be past, present, or future: and similar temporally forward and backward functional relations are seen in many inorganic mechanisms. If it be thought that there can be consciousness without behavior, I would say that the doctrine of dynamogenesis, and indeed the doctrine of psycho-physical parallelism itself, assert just the contrary. Of course muscle tonus and 'motor set' are as much behavior as is the more extensive play of limb. In short, I know not what distinction can be drawn between the object of consciousness and the object of behavior.

Again, if the object of which behavior is a constant function is the object of consciousness, *that function of it which behavior is* presents a close parallel to volition. Psychological theory has never quite succeeded in making will a content of knowledge in the same sense as sensation, perception, and thought; the heterogeneous (motor-image) theory being manifestly untrue to rather the larger part of will acts. Indeed, in the strict sense the theory of innervation feelings is the only one which ever allowed will to be, in its own right, a content. All other views, including the heterogeneous, show one's knowledge of one's own will acts to be gained by a combination of memory and the direct observation of what one's own *body is doing*. And this is quite in harmony with the idea that what one wills is that which one's body does (in attitude or overt act) toward the environment. In a larger sense, however, and with less deference to the tendencies of bead theorizing, one's volitions are obviously identical with that which one's body in the capacity of released mechanism *does*. If a man avoids draughts, that is both the behavior and the volition at once, and any motor-image, 'fiat,' or other account of it merely substitutes some subordinate aspect for that which is the immediate volition.*

The case is somewhat different if we inquire what in behavior corresponds to the 'knower' of the cognitive relation. Clearly this knower can be nothing but the body itself; for behaviorism, the body is aware, the body acts. But this body will hardly take the place, in many minds, of that metaphysical 'subject' which has been thought to be

* Cf. "The Concept of Consciousness," 1914, Chap. XIV.

the very nucleolus of the ego. Yet something can be said for the neuro-muscular organism in the capacity of cognitive subject.* In so far as the 'subject' is supposed to serve as the center of perception and apperception and guarantor of the 'unity' of consciousness, the central nervous system will serve admirably. In fact it is, precisely, a perdurable central exchange where messages from the outer world meet and react on one another and on 'the so-to-say stored stimuli,' and whence the return impulses emerge. Furthermore it is securely established that by just as much as this central nervous exchange has its unity impaired, by just so much is the unity of apperception (including the 'transcendental') impaired. Dissociation of the neural complex means dissociation of personality, cognitive as well as volitional. Again, in so far as the metaphysical 'subject' is defined as the 'necessary correlate' of the object in knowledge, the body may well serve this function. For in the response relation, as above defined, it does precisely this: without the body the outer object would obviously never become the *object* of behavior. And

* We shall consider the soul as essence of personality further on.

should otherwise the response relation turn out to be the cognitive relation, the physical organism will necessarily take its place as 'correlate of the object,' and supersede the metaphysical subject. I am not aware that this 'subject' has ever served any other actually empirical wants, useful as it may be in the higher flights of speculation. And one recalls that of this more transcendental aspect of the 'subject' James said, that "the 'Self of selves,' when carefully examined, is found to consist mainly of the collection of these peculiar motions in the head or between the head and throat." * It will be recalled, too, that so faithful an idealist as Schopenhauer found reason to declare that "the philosophers who set up a *soul* as this metaphysical kernel, i.e., an originally and essentially *knowing* being," have made a *false assertion*. For, he goes on to say, "knowing is a secondary function and conditioned by the organism, just like any other." † I venture to predict that behaviorism will be able to give a complete account of cognition without invoking the services of the

* William James, "Principles of Psychology," Vol. I, p. 301.

† Schopenhauer, "The World as Will and Idea," Vol. II, Chap. XIX. (Eng. transl., 1886, Vol. II, p. 462.)

RESPONSE AND COGNITION 177

'metaphysical subject' nor of any one of its swarming progeny of Ego's.

We have seen that behavior, as " any process of release which is a function of factors external to the mechanism released," in so far accounts for the phenomena of cognition that it provides a content of knowledge, a willer, and a knower. Let us now consider it in respect to three remaining psychological phenomena: attention, feeling, and personality.

Attention is the most difficult of these topics, and the problem resolves itself, to my mind, the most neatly: this problem being, What in behavior would correspond to attention in cognition? Suppose, however, that we first ask, What in the attention of empirical psychology corresponds to 'attention' as understood by the more or less still-current faculty and rational psychologies? These latter say that the 'soul' is unitary, and that it 'attends' to one 'idea' at a time, or to a unified group of 'ideas.' It follows that there are 'ideas' to which the soul is not attending; also, quite inevitably, that attention is the act of attending. *Bon!* On the empirical side we have attention as " the taking possession by the mind, in clear and

vivid form, of one out of what seem several simultaneously possible objects or trains of thought." *
The essentials in this definition are will, clearness or vividness (degrees of consciousness), selection (or its converse, inhibition). The volitional element in behavioristic attention will be, as we have already seen, the process whereby the *body* assumes and exercises an adjustment or motor set such that its activities are some function of an object; are focused on an object. The selection or inhibition factor has already been so unanimously explained in terms of neuro-muscular augmentation and inhibition that I need not dwell on it further. Clearness, vividness, or *degree of consciousness* is the crux. And this is in fact what the faculty and rationalistic accounts of attention have come down to in empirical psychology.

It would be unfair to say that empirical psychology has now merely renamed attention, and called it ' clearness.' It has analyzed the faculty of ' attention,' and by separating out the factors

* James, "Principles of Psychology," Vol. I, pp. 403-4. In this definition James has summed up with singular brevity *all* the factors which have persistently maintained their place in the historical development of attention.

(volitional, etc.) that belong elsewhere, it has found the core in ' clearness,' or, better, grades of consciousness. But I cannot see that empirical psychology has done more than this. It teaches that there are degrees of being conscious; and this is a singular doctrine, for it goes much against the grain to say that an idea can be more or less conscious. From the nature of the case introspection cannot help here,* for one cannot attend to an idea of any of the lesser grades of clearness, *idem est*, to an idea which is not attended to. The notion savors of Spencer's 'Unknowable,' of which he knew so much. In an acute discussion of this concept Barker says: " When it is said that clearness is a simple and indefinable attribute comparable with quality, intensity, extension, and duration, I simply do not find in the statement the description of anything which I can recognize in my own experience." † I bring forward these considerations in order not to disparage the ' clearness ' doctrine, but to show, if possible, exactly what it is that

* Certain introspective investigations to the contrary notwithstanding. I recommend the reader to consult these. Cf. Titchener, "Lectures on the Elementary Psychology of Feeling and Attention," 1908, pp. 211 *et seq*.

† H. Barker, Proceedings of the Aristotelian Society, 1912-13, Vol. XIII, p. 270.

behaviorism must account for if it is to account for attention.

Now there are psychological phenomena which have seemed to argue for this notion of 'clearness.' The first is that ideas come into consciousness and go out of it, and that this process is oftentimes, apparently, not instantaneous. Ideas recede before they vanish, as objects recede in space: a sort of consciousness perspective. And this variation is not in the dimension of intensity. But this observable waxing and waning of ideas may be otherwise interpreted than as grades of consciousness. On the basis of a psychological atomism (otherwise an inevitable doctrine) this so-called 'clearness' dimension would come down to the thesis that the atomic elements occur in groups of various degrees of organization; that the most coherently organized groups are the 'clear' or 'vivid' states (or ideas); that the elements, which themselves are either *in* or *not* in 'consciousness,' enter consciousness unorganized and are there built up into 'clear' states; and that again these clear states more or less disintegrate before their component elements pass out of consciousness. It has always seemed to me that this view, which is of course not new, squares perfectly with the phenomena of fringe of consciousness; and with the intently observed fading of images. In this way 'attention' would be reduced not to the 'attribute of clearness,' but to the process of organization and deorganization of content-atoms. I find nothing in Leibnitz, to whom the doctrine of clearness and obscurity in ideas owes so much, which would oppose this interpretation.

Now if attention is found to be such a process, then our view of behavior not merely allows for, but it *predicts* the attention process. Any complex form of behavior is, of course, organized out of simpler responses, which do not always slip into the higher form of integration instantaneously. Their more or less gradual organization is the process of attention. One sits down unguardedly in a public waiting-room, and presently one's train of thought is interrupted by 'something,' which changes almost instantly to 'something I am sitting upon.' This already has involved a very different motor attitude from that in force, while one was idly whiling the time away. At this juncture, if one brings the entire faculty of attention to bear on the 'something,' taking care, however, not to move one's body, for this would bring in a multitude of new peripheral data, I do not think that this 'something' will gain in 'clearness.' It may, however, change to ' extra pressure at a point on the underside of my thigh.' Here, it seems to me, if one still does not move, all the 'attention' possible will not make this pressure 'clearer'; it is such an intensity of pressure, and there it is. Next, this pressure will probably change back to 'something,' and 'something' will change to 'pocketbook,' 'gold ring,' 'sticky piece of candy, 'apple core,' 'soiled handkerchief,'—each involving a new motor attitude; as one is soon convinced if 'something' happens to change to 'possibly a snake.' If new peripheral data are admitted, of course the search for enhanced 'clearness' in the originally given piece of content is even more complicated and dubious. The commonly alleged cases of increased ' clearness' are cases of augmented sensory data (producing greater specificity of attitude); this is flagrantly so in the often-cited transition of an object from peripheral to foveal vision. Here the series may be 'something,' spot, gray spot, yellow-gray spot, yellow irregular spot, yellow sort of semicircular thing, yellowish-orange dome-shaped object, orange dome-shaped bright object with irregularity at top, orange lamp-shade, lighted lamp with orange shade, on table. But this is not increased 'clearness.' Here, as before, the response attitude has steadily changed (and developed). I have tried for years to find a plausible instance of changing 'clearness' or 'vividness' and for evidence of 'levels of attention'; but the search has been in vain.

According to the clearness doctrine, even when a content is built up to greater definition and detail (Leibnitz's 'distinctness') by the addition of new components, the original elements ought presumably to gain in clearness. But the general tendency seems to be, rather, that they actually disappear. A first glance at an unfamiliar object usually yields salient features like color and form; under attentive observation the content develops into a thing of higher interest in which, unless there are special reasons wherefor they remain important, form and color are lost. An archeologist will soon lose ('pay no attention to') the color or mere contour of a new find which he is intently studying. A jeweler would probably remain conscious of the color of a new gem which he is examining; but here it should seem that this color, if it changes at all, does not gain 'clearness,' but a definite nuance; which is a very different matter. Interest, '*Aufgabe*' and '*Bewusstseinslage*' (which are the psychologist's names for motor set) determine what shall come or go, and how contents shall develop.

But not all psychologists interpret attention in terms of 'clearness.' This latter is an attribute of content, and there is a tendency in several independent quarters to assign to process, or some aspect of process, various phenomena which have been in the past referred to content. The interpretation of attention, not as 'clearness,' but as the organization process of psychic elements (as above described), is a familiar case in point. The 'imageless thought' movement is another. Associationism described thought as the interaction of content units ('ideas'), while this theory describes it as interplay without content. Again the various groups of thinkers who employ the now-familiar *clichés* of 'act,' '*psychischer Akt*,' and '*psychische Funktion*' are tending in the same direction; that is, toward emphasizing process of consciousness more than content. Now I should be far from arguing that there can be interplay without ideas as the basis of it. Such a thing seems to me untrue to fact, and in theory I can understand it no more than I can how there should be motion with nothing to move, or relation with no entities to be related. But I mention this tendency to emphasize process, only in order to point out that however much of it shall turn out to be empirically valid, so much behaviorism will find no trouble in taking care of.* For the responding mechanism presents any amount of process; all too much, indeed. For both content and process of cognition the specific response relation has a place.

A further aspect of attention remains unconsidered. This is attention at its lowest or 'unconscious' stage. Even should attention generally be found to consist not in a clearness attribute, but in degrees of organization of content, there would still remain to be accounted for those facts which so persistently through the history of psychology have kept alive the distinction of conscious and unconscious, the latter being again distinct from

* Cf., in this connection, the brilliant work of N. Kostyleff, "Le Mécanisme cérébral de la pensée," Paris, 1914.

'mere cerebration.' This distinction, obscure and disputed and yet invincible as it has been, becomes luminously construed and wholly justified if cognition is identified with the behavior relation. With the establishment of the first specific response, out of the integration of reflexes, there is of course content (of an atomic, elementary order, very possibly). But this content could never be identified with brain, nor with cerebration: for it is that object or aspect of the *environment, to which* the brain reflexes are adjusted, *of which* they are now constant functions. What will happen, now, to these elementary objective contents when these primitive specific responses are still further integrated into more elaborate forms of behavior? They will obviously not turn into 'cerebration,' for they are aspects of the environment. Well, what in fact happens, in such a case, to consciousness? When one first learned to walk, the process involved lively consciousness of pressure on the soles, and at different intensities in the two feet; of visible objects which one carefully watched in order to steady oneself, etc., etc. One now walks with head in air and in almost total oblivion of the steadying visual objects and the unfeeling tactual objects with sharp corners, the stairs and the inclines, which it was once so wise to keep in view. At first one stepped, and each step was an adventure in itself; now one *walks*, or perhaps not consciously even this; for one may consciously not be walking or running, but catching a train, thinking over a lecture, bracing oneself to do a sharp stroke of business. The walking behavior, although no less behavior and no less involving functional adjustment toward the environment and hence no less involving ' content,' has now been taken up (along with other behavior systems) and made component of a more highly integrated and elaborate form of behavior. This latter it now serves. And the object or objective situation to which the latter is a functional adjustment is almost always more and more remote from the immediate momentary *stimuli* than are the objects of which the component systems are functions. For the behavior relation *all* of the environmental aspects to which the organism is in any wise responding are content; all are ' in consciousness.' But what portion of all this, then, is the ' attentive consciousness,' the upper level of personal awareness? Why, obviously, the upper level consists of that object or system of objects to which the *upper level* of integrated behavior is specifically adjusted. *The attentive level of consciousness, that of which the 'self' is aware, is that most comprehensive environmental field to which the organism has so far attained (by integration) the capacity to respond.** The attentive level at any particular moment is the most comprehensive field to which the organism is at that moment specifically responding (of which its behavior is a function). All other aspects of the environment, to which the ancillary and component behavior systems are at the time responding, are 'coconscious,' 'subconscious,' 'unconscious'—as you prefer; but they are not brain, nor cerebration, nor neurogramme. They are in consciousness, but not in the upper field of attention. In other words, the most highly integrated behavior system that is in action determines the personal level of attention. If I stop 'thinking about' (comprehensively responding to) the forthcoming business engagement to which my legs are now carrying me, I can consciously walk; if I cease this, I can *consciously* take a single step; ceasing

* Cf. Knight Dunlap, "An Outline of Psychobiology." Baltimore, 1914, p. 114.

RESPONSE AND COGNITION 189

this I can *consciously* merely equilibrate in an erect posture; ceasing this I become *conscious* of pressure on the soles of my two feet. The one change in this series has been the steady reduction in the comprehensiveness of my bodily response. The 'stream of consciousness' is nothing but this selected procession of environmental aspects to which the body's ever-varying motor adjustments are directed.*

This explains, as no other view has ever explained, the relation of automatic or habitual to conscious activities. Habitual activities are usually performed below the attentive level, because as soon as any behavior system is organized ('learned') the organism *goes on* to integrate this, together with others, into some more comprehensive system; and concomitantly the first mentioned system sinks into the field of the coconscious or unconscious. This is the purpose of education, the meaning of development. On the other hand, there seems to be no, even the most simple and habitual, activity that cannot, and, on occasion, is not, performed *consciously*. What the organism

* I shall attempt at an early date to show how successfully this view replaces the association doctrine.

shall be aware of depends solely on what it is doing; and it can do anything which it ever learned to do, whether complex or simple. The remarkable harmony between this view and the facts is brought out if one turns to the other views. One theory, for instance, has it that the cerebral cortex is the 'seat of consciousness,' while habituated unconscious acts are done by the cerebellum and cord. From which it follows that when a motion is first learned (for this appears to be always a conscious process) it is learned by the cerebrum, but thereafter it is performed by the cerebellum and cord (which never learned it). A most plausible conception! And thereafter, since it can be performed either consciously or unconsciously, a double set of nervous mechanisms is maintained in readiness! Or again, there is a view that ' consciousness ' is comparable to resistance, or heat, developed at neural cell or synapse. Unconsciousness in a process is attained when the neural path is worn so ' smooth ' that no appreciable heat is developed.* When, then, an act has once become automatic it *cannot* be performed consciously, unless the organism relearns it

* This view, or some variation of it, has been advocated by Spencer, Romanes, Mercier, Wm. McDougall, and others.

in a new set of nerves. This patently violates the facts.*

Lastly, in leaving this view of the attentive level and the coconscious levels, I must drop the hint that it will be found to throw a flood of light on the otherwise Cimmerian darkness that now surrounds 'unconscious sensations,' 'unconscious judgments,' and 'illusions of judgment'; not to mention more modern categories such as '*Aufgabe*,' '*Bewusstseinslage*,' Freud's upper and lower 'instances,' and double personality with all its allied problems. Nothing could be more inspiriting to a believer in the purely objective psychology, if dejected, than to read in the light of our definition of behavior what Weber, for instance, had to say about '*stellvertretender Verstand*,' † or again Euler, Helmholtz, Hering, or Mach about 'unconscious judgments'; such vistas of unforced and lucid explanation are here opened out.

Another phenomenon that seems to be more or less universally involved in cognition is feeling, and

* Cf. E. B. Holt, "The Concept of Consciousness," 1914, p. 324 *et seq.*

† E. H. Weber, "Der Tastsinn und das Gemeingefühl," 1846, in Wagner's "Handwörterbuch der Physiologie," Bd. III, S. 484 *et seq.*

our question is whether the behavior relation makes such a phenomenon intelligible. Here, again, psychology is not very clear as to how the phenomenon is to be described. The early view that feelings are two content elements—pleasantness and unpleasantness—gave way first to the idea that feelings are two opposed attributes of content, making one distinct dimension comparable with intensity (the 'feeling-tone' theory). Then more recently there has been a marked tendency (which was indeed adumbrated much earlier), as in the case of attention, to refer the phenomenon to process rather than to content, because it seems certain that pleasantness is essentially connected with enhanced, unpleasantness with diminished, consciousness and activity. Some degree of avoidance inevitably attends the unpleasant, and so forth; and on the other hand, it seems impossible to lay hold of any distinct pleasantness or unpleasantness 'content.'.*

* The only recent theory which I know, that of Titchener, which definitely makes feeling a content, at the same time declares it to lack the 'attribute of clearness'; while other psychologists, as Münsterberg, declare that a content which lacks this attribute *ipso facto* ceases to exist. Wundt's tridimensional theory appears to make feeling either a kinesthetic *sensation*, or else a function thereof (i.e., not a content, but a *process*).

One thing, which from the behavioristic point of view seems obvious, is that feeling is some modification of response which is determined by factors *within* the organism. No dependable and direct correspondence between feeling phenomena and the environment appears. This fact was noted extremely early, and has indeed often served as a clinching argument for the subjectivist point of view. But if one considers what the organism is— a vast congeries of microscopic cells, and each one a chemical process which is practically never in exact equilibrium, whose very use, indeed, involves a disturbance of any even relative equilibrium, where, further, the whole is at every moment both absorbing and disbursing energy of several kinds—then it becomes downright unthinkable that in any behavior which such an organism succeeds in evolving, the constant functions which this is of objects in the environment *should not* be further complicated by variant factors contained in the mechanisms which are maintaining these functions; just as the constant of gravity is complicated by skin friction, wind, and other forces which act on falling bodies. The phenomenon of 'feeling' is predictable from our definition of behavior and a rudimentary acquaintance with living tissue. Where in the organism the feeling process is to be sought, or in which aspect of neuro-muscular interplay, cannot, I think, be advisedly inquired until the phenomenon has been more exactly *described*. Meanwhile behaviorism is embarrassed, not by the difficulty of explaining feeling, but by the very wealth of alternative which it finds at its disposal. It can well afford to wait until psychologists get something that at least resembles a scientific description of that which they call 'feeling.' Meanwhile the closer they have come to anything exact, the nearer they have come to the position above outlined. Such a theory as that of Meyer* is straight behaviorism.

It is interesting to note that if, according to our definition of behavior, feeling is a complication that the organism as such introduces in the function which behavior is of the environment, we see immediately why feeling is not unrelated to stimulus and why it is closely related to will. Feelings are more or less, but *never infallibly*, determined by the stimuli. If one gives simultaneously two 'incon-

* M. Meyer, "The Nervous Correlate of Pleasantness and Unpleasantness," *Psychol. Rev.*, 1908, XV, pp. 201-216; 292-322.

gruous' stimuli, the organism commonly 'feels unpleasantness,' which is due, if appearances are not deceptive, to the interferences which each stimulus exerts on the response which the other alone would have called forth. Introspectively one says, "Those two things do not harmonize, they conflict," or in observing another organism one says, "Its responses are impeded." Now it is *within* the organism that these stimuli interfere, and only by reason of the existence and idiosyncrasies of the organism that they do interfere. Thus feeling is a complication of response due to factors within the organism. It is now clear why 'feeling' is not found in the evolutionary series lower than where 'behavior' is found. As the subjectivist is so fond of saying, " None but a 'conscious' creature can feel." 'Tis true.

And again, if feeling is an internally determined modification of the behavior function and this latter, as previously explained, is the will, it is clear enough why feeling and will are bound to be concomitant phenomena. And whatever empirical truth there may be in the 'pleasure-pain theory' of will will find ample recognition and explanation in this fact. It shows, too, why will is possible without feeling, while feeling is not possible without will.* And once again, if will is behavior that is function of an object, and feeling is an *ex machina* 'Nuancirung' of this function, while the 'content of consciousness' is the outer *object* to which the behavior function is directed, one sees how a confusion might arise as to whether feeling was a 'Nuancirung' of the motor attitude or of the object of that attitude. That such a confusion is prevalent is shown by James in his essay, "The Place of Affectional Facts in a World of Pure Experience." †

We come, lastly, to what is called 'personality' and the behavior relation. I have already pointed out that for behaviorism will is that function which the organism's behavior is of the object. These various functions are of different degrees of integration, and in a well-knit character they have become organized (as fast as each developed) with

---

* A disputed point, of course. I believe that the facts (and an adequate conception of the will) quite support my statement. In such a word as 'apathetic,' which should refer to feeling alone, the notion of feeling has been actually superseded by that of will.

† This *Journal*, Vol. II, pp. 281-287. And 'pathetic' has thus come to refer to the object, the situation.

one another into higher forms of behavior, and if this process has not been thwarted by untoward circumstance, they are at every period of life integrated to date. That is to say, there is at any moment of life *some* course of action (behavior) which enlists *all* of the capacities of the organism: this is phrased voluntaristically as 'some interest or aim to which a man devotes all his powers,' to which ' his whole being is consecrated.' This matter of the unthwarted lifelong progress of behavior integration is of profound importance, for it is the transition from behavior to conduct, and to *moral conduct*. The more integrated behavior is harmonious and consistent behavior toward a larger and more comprehensive situation, toward a bigger section of the universe; it is lucidity and breadth of purpose. And it is wonderful to observe how with every step in 'this process the bare scientific *description* of *what the organism does* approaches more and more to a description of moral conduct. In short, all of the more embracing behavior formulæ (functions) are moral. The behaviorist has not changed his strictly empirical, objective procedure one iota, and he has scientifically observed the evolution of reflex process into morality.

The reader shall illustrate this for himself. Take *any* instance of wrong conduct as, say, a child's playing with fire, and consider why it is wrong and how must it change to become right. It is wrong simply because it is behavior that does not take into account consequences; it is not adjusted to *enough* of the environment; it will be made right by an enlargement of its scope and reach. This is just what the integration of specific responses effects; and through it, as I have remarked previously, the immediate stimulus (ever the bugbear of moralists) recedes further and further from view.

The entire psychology of Freud is a discussion of the miscarriages which occur in this lifelong process of integration, their causes and remedies. Freud believes, and seems to have proven, that thwarted integration (called by some 'dissociation') is responsible for a large part of mental and nervous disease. For Freud's 'wish' is precisely that thing which in my definition of behavior I call 'function'; it is that motor set of the organism which, if opposed by other motor sets, is functional attitude toward the environment, and which, if unopposed, actuates the organism to overt behavior

which is a constant function of the environment.*
The evil resulting from thwarted integration is
'suppression'—where one motor set becomes organically opposed to another, the two are dissociated and the personality is split: whereas the
two should have been harmoniously knit together,
coöperating to produce behavior which is yet more
far-reachingly adapted to the environment. The
sane man is the man who (however limited the
scope of his behavior) has no such suppression
incorporated in him. The wise man must be sane,
and must have scope as well.

A further and important conclusion which I believe has not yet been drawn, but which follows
necessarily from Freud's behavioristic psychology
(for such it is), is that only the sane man is good
and only the sane man is free. For the man with
suppressions is capable of no act which some part
of his own nature does not oppose, and none which
this now suppressed part will not probably some
day in overt act undo. There is no course of
action into which he can throw his whole energy,
nothing which he can 'wish' to do which he does

* The reader will find a fuller account of this view of
will, morals, and function in my chapter on Volition in
"The Concept of Consciousness."

not wish, to some extent and at the same time, not to do. Thus he can never do the 'good' unreservedly, never without secret rebellion 'in his heart.' And such a man is not good. In the same way he is never free, for all that he would do is hindered, and usually, in fact, frustrated, by his own other self. This fact, so brief in the statement, has been copiously illustrated by Freud and is extraordinarily illuminating to one who is trying to observe and to understand human conduct at large. One soon sees that in the most literal sense there is no impediment to man's freedom except a self-contained and internal one. In thus showing that virtue and freedom derive from the same source Freud and behaviorism have empirically confirmed that doctrine of freedom which Socrates and Plato propounded, and which even religion has deemed too exalted for human nature's daily food—the doctrine that only the good man is free.*

Such for behaviorism is the personality or the soul. It is the attitude and conduct, *idem est*, the purposes, of the body. In those happy individuals in whom the daily integration of behavior is suc-

* Freud's verification of this is far more complete than in my brief outline.

cessfully accomplished the soul is a unit and a moral unit. In others in whom the integration has been frustrated the soul is not a unit, but a collection of warring factions seated in one distracted body. Such a creature has not one soul, but many, and misses of morals and of freedom by exactly as much as it has missed of unity, that is, of the progressive integration of its behavior. According to this view the soul is not substantial and not corporeal; but it is concrete, definite, empirically observable, and in a living body incorporated—a true 'entelechy.' With such a doctrine of personality and the soul as this, behaviorism can rest unperturbed while the sad procession of Spirits, Ghost-Souls, 'transcendental' Egos, and what not, passes by and vanishes in its own vapor. For all of these are contentless monads, and they have no windows. In fine, for behaviorism there is one unbroken integration series from reflex action, to behavior, conduct, moral conduct, and the unified soul.

In the first part of this article I expressed the opinion that behaviorists have not fully realized the significance of what they are doing because, while in practice they have discarded it, in theory they still, like most psychologists, adhere to the 'bead theory' of causation. Now their opponents, who believe in 'consciousness' and a subjective soul-principle, are equally addicted to another view of causation, the teleological. This view, however, which indeed does justice to a feature of causation which the bead theory ignores, is equally wide of the truth. The functional view combines and reconciles the two, and accounts for 'teleology.' This is why the behaviorist who, whatever his theory, *practices* the functional view, finds in his phenomena no residue of unexplained 'teleological' behavior. For brevity I must let a single illustration suffice to show this. Why does a boy go fishing? The bead theory says, because of something in his 'previous state.' The teleological theory says, because of an 'idea of end' in his 'mind' (subjective categories). The functional theory says, because the behavior of the growing organism is so far integrated as to respond specifically to such an environmental object as fish in the pond. It, too, admits that the boy's 'thought' (content) is the fish. But now a mere attitude or motor set could condition the same 'idea of end'—the fish—and it need go no further; so that the 'idea of end' has no causal efficacy whatsoever. This latter is supplied by that further influx of nervous energy which touches off the motor set and makes it go over into overt behavior. The whole truth of teleology is taken up, and rectified, in that objective reference which behavior as *function of an object* provides for. It is to be empirically noted otherwise that the 'idea of end' is totally inefficacious causally, for *more often than not* it is merely an *idée fixe,* which indicates the presence of an habitually aimless and irresolute will.

III. CONCLUSION

In the foregoing pages I have offered what I believe to be a somewhat more exact definition of behavior or specific response than any that I have previously met, and have attempted to show that this behavior relation, objective and definite as it is, can lay considerable claim to being the long-sought cognitive relation between 'subject' and object. For my own part I make no doubt that the cognitive relation is this, although my definition of behavior may have to be overhauled and improved in the light of future empirical discoveries. It follows that I believe the future of psychology, human as well as animal, to lie in the hands of the behaviorists and of those who may decide to join them. I wish to add a word on the pragmatic aspect of the objective movement in psychology and philosophy.

So far as modern philosophy goes it seems to me that the several present-day tendencies to resolve the subjective category of soul-substance into objective relations all take their origin in the contentions of the eighteenth-century materialists. In this the writings of the French and English ideologists, sensationalists, and other empiricists (including such naturalists as Charles Bonnet) have not been without influence. One might even find, for instance, a behaviorist's charter in the following words of Joseph Priestley: " I cannot imagine that a human body, completely organized, and having life, would want sensation and thought. This I suppose to follow, *of course*, as much as the circulation of the blood follows respiration." *

In the actual present this objective tendency is represented by groups of men whose interests are otherwise so divergent that it may not be amiss to point out their fundamental unanimity of aim.

* "Disquisitions Relating to Matter and Spirit," 2d edition, 1782, Vol. I, section XIII, p. 151.

There are at least four such groups—the American realists, the English realists, the French and Russian 'objective' psychologists, and the 'behaviorists.' I think that it would not be difficult to persuade the Freudians that they, too, are objectivists —a fifth group. Possibly the Pragmatists would be another. And I should have mentioned Radical Empiricists at the top of the list if I detected the existence of any such group.

The American realists have been so explicitly conscious of their aim to abolish the subjective ('consciousness,' etc.) and to interpret mental phenomena in an objective relational manner, and they have written so often in this very *Journal*, that I need say nothing further. It would be unjust of me, without very careful study, to attempt to weigh the individual contributions of these realists, but I must say in passing that in the early, very lean and hungry years of American realism yeoman's service was rendered by Professors Woodbridge and Montague. At the present time all of these realists, for their number is no longer merely 'Six,' seem definitely to have escaped the 'egocentric predicament' and to have repudiated the 'subjective, as such.' It seems to me that they stand in need of a positive theory of cognition, and that they will find this if they will consider the ways of the patient animal-behaviorist. Cognition exists in the animals, and there in its simpler and more analyzable forms.

The English 'realists' are all, so far as I can see, Cartesian dualists of one complexion or another. But they are all, or nearly all, animated by the desire to be released from the bondage of subjectivism. In so far they have a common aim with the American realists, and might find it worth while to examine cognition in its infrahuman forms.

The Russian and French objective psychologists are determined, just as James has urged and as the behaviorist is doing, to abandon the ghost-soul. They are further determined to discover all the phenomena of consciousness in some or other reflex processes. If they succeed, theirs is clearly bound to be a relational theory of consciousness. And they are thus the natural allies of all realists.

The behaviorists themselves are, as I have said, *in practice* the one great luminary of the psychologic sky. In theory they need, I think, as in this present paper I have tried to outline, an exact definition of what behavior is. They are to-day in danger of making the materialist's error, of denying the *facts*, as well as the theory, of consciousness. Thus Bethe, in his fascinating book " Dürfen wir den Ameisen und Bienen psychische Qualitäten zuschreiben?" * describes much of the complex behavior of ants and bees exactly (and in the sense which I have previously commended), but then adds that, *since* we can explain all these phenomena in terms of reflex process, we have no right to 'impute consciousness' to these little creatures. He fails to see that he has been describing consciousness. This method, pursued, would end by picking out the single reflex components of human behavior, neglecting the equally important relations in which they are organized, and by then concluding that there is no such thing as sensation, perception, or thought. Just as one might accurately describe each wheel of a watch, and then conclude that it is not a timepiece; ' time ' not being visible in any one of the wheels. But this would be to miss altogether that novelty which arises during the integration of reflex process into behavior. As I have tried to show, behaviorism is neither subjectivism, nor, on the other hand, is it materialism (in

* Bonn, 1898.

the accepted sense of that term—the sense, that is, in which the facts of consciousness are slurred over or even repudiated outright).

As to the others, it is my belief that both the Freudians and the pragmatists will find a number of baffling points in their own systems explained, and these systems extended and fortified, if they will consider whether cognition *for them* is not essentially contained within the behavior relation.*
That this is true for Freudianism I shall attempt to demonstrate in the near future.

In fine, it should seem that a fundamental unity of purpose animates the investigators of these several groups, although they approach the question of cognition from very different directions. Will it not be a source of strength for all if they can manage to keep a sympathetic eye on the methods and the discoveries of one another?

---

* I would commend to them Professor John B. Watson's valiant and clear-headed volume, "Behavior" (New York, 1914); also Professor Wm. McDougall's very instructive "Social Psychology" (London, 1914), although this latter with more reserve since it is not untainted with subjectivism.

INDEX

INDEX

Appetite, 107 f.
Aristotle, 49, 95, 97, 135, 140
Attention, 177 ff.

Bead theory, 157, 160 f., 169 f., 201 f.
Behavior, 52 ff., 68, 78 f., 87 f., 91, 125, 155 f., 160 ff., 164 ff., 167, 177, 206 f.

Censor, 14, 16, 27 f.
Character, 7, 13, 28 f., 196 f.
Cognition, 82, 96 f., 99, 171 ff., 203
Conduct, 4, 101, 132, 197 f.
Conflict (*see also* Dilemma), 5, 125 ff., 137 f., 195
Content of consciousness, 47, 97, 155 f., 172 f., 186 ff.

Darwin, Charles, 20, 61 f.
Dilemma, 111, 115, 118 ff., 130 f., 136.
Discrimination, 123 f., 127 f., 134 f., 142, 148
Dissociation, 105, 128
Dreams, 5 ff.
Dynamic psychology, 4, 47

Ego complex, 13, 24, 35, 37 f., 115 f., 147
Energy, 4, 20
Ethics (*see also* Morality), 100 ff., 112, 132 f., 141, 148 ff.

Feeling, 191 ff.
Freedom, 140 ff., 200 f.

Hegel, 135 ff.

Incoherence, 7 f., 121
Integration, 118, 122, 142, 145 ff., 155, 165, 196 f., 201
Interference, 5, 7, 31, 63 f., 68, 74 f., 127
Introspection, 57, 83, 87 f., 91

James, William, 61, 69, 71, 89, 176, 178, 196
Jones, Dr. Ernest, 32

Knower, 174 ff.

Language, 110
Learning, 69 ff., 74, 101 ff., 106

Mephistopheles, 143, 147
Morality, 147 f.
Moral sanction, 105 f., 109, 112 f., 124, 130 ff., 141, 151, 198
Motor attitude, 4, 59 ff., 94, 97 f., 173

Plato, 139 ff., 200
Priestley, 204
Prince, Dr. Morton, 45

Realpolitik, 151
Remorse, 11, 14 f.
Response, 49 f.

Schadenfreude, 22, 26, 37
Schopenhauer, 176

INDEX

Sexual appetite, iv, 108
Sleep, 14
Slips of the pen or tongue, 32 ff.
Socrates, 139 ff., 200
Soul, 49, 65, 95, 118, 142, 176, 200 f.
Specific response, 52 ff., 58, 76, 153 ff., 188
Spinoza, 60, 81
Stimulus, recession of, 75 ff., 80, 91 f., 164 f., 187
Subconscious, 31, 40, 88, 144, 185 ff., 191
Suppression, 5, 17, 27 f., 37, 101, 105, 118, 120, 127 f., 132, 142, 199
Symbolism, 10
Sympathy, 22, 107

Teleology, 54, 56, 59, 65 f., 93 ff., 100 f., 108 f., 132, 162, 202 f.
Thomas, 140
Thought and will are one, 6, 60 f., 81, 98, 125, 131
Thought-transference, 40
Truthfulness, 30 f., 112 f., 114, 117

Virtue, 125, 132, 135, 140 ff., 147, 197 f.

Will, 95, 139 ff., 173 f., 195 f.
Wish, 3 (defined), 48 f., 56 f., 59, 94 f., 99 f., 131, 151, 198
Wit, 17 ff.

www.ingramcontent.com/pod-product-compliance
Lightning Source LLC
LaVergne TN
LVHW051728080426
835511LV00018B/2947